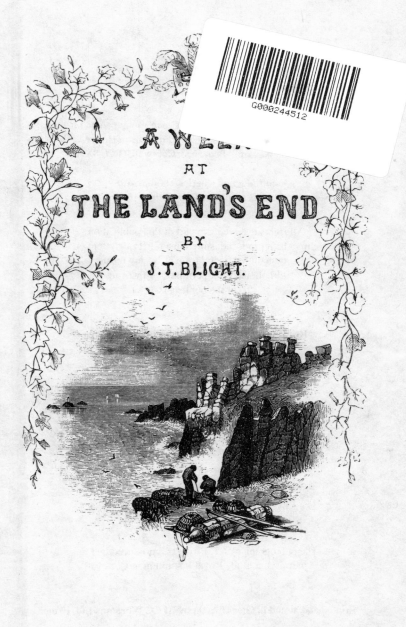

A WEEK

AT

THE LAND'S END

BY

J.T. BLIGHT.

First published in 1861 by Longman, Green, Longman and Roberts.
This edition published in 1989 by Alison Hodge,
Bosulval, Newmill, Penzance, Cornwall TR20 8XA.

British Library Cataloguing in Publication Data

Blight, J.T. (John Thomas)
A week at the Land's End.
1. Cornwall. Penwith (District). Description & travel
– 1837–1901
I. Title
914.23'750481

ISBN 0-906720-20-6

Printed and bound in Great Britain by BPCC Wheatons Ltd, Exeter.

INTRODUCTION TO THE 1989 EDITION

JOHN THOMAS BLIGHT's career has been described as 'tragic and enigmatic'. Tragic, certainly, as to its latter part; but the principal enigmas (the course of his last forty years and the true date of his death) have been resolved. While we cannot and should not forget all this latter period, Blight himself will be (and should be) remembered in the context of his work. His *Land's End*, the happiest of his books, is now re-launched and can meet with nothing save praise. Before assessing it, we must consider the man himself.

The surname Blight is pretty generally distributed throughout Cornwall. An earlier, and possibly parallel, form of it was 'Bligh' (as with Admiral William 'Breadfruit' Bligh of the *Bounty*, himself of Cornish stock) or 'Bleigh', and indeed the name was sometimes spoken as 'Blee' in west Cornwall. Robert Blight, born at St Germans in 1804, married and removed to Redruth; here John Thomas Blight was born in October 1835, followed by his brother Joseph in 1837. Not long after this Blight senior obtained a position as a private schoolmaster at Jordan House, Penzance. A man of talent and of natural curiosity, he contributed to the *West Briton* and to local journals numerous articles on antiquities of West Cornwall. Today, he would have led rambles and published guided walks. In the 1850s his influence upon his two small sons, as they grew up and accompanied him, was profound. Joseph, who became a professional illustrator, left Cornwall for London. J.T.B., as we can call him, may not have been a Penzance man by birth, but in retrospect we see him as *the* reflector and chronicler of rural West Penwith in the mid-Victorian era.

In strictly mundane terms, J.T.B. never had a job (unless we except some reported part-time work as an assistant librarian). He clearly intended to live by his pen, combining a draughtsman's art with the literary skills of an educated, slightly romantic, young man whose family could support him. Blight's interests, if listed in contemporary language, embraced botany and natural history, ecclesiology, and antiquarian topics of all kinds. He was hardly out of his teens before a deserved repute as an accurate and knowledgeable engraver led to commissions. It also introduced J.T.B. to circles of learning and polite literature; to clerical men like William Iago and R.S. Hawker, landowners and persons from county families such as Augustus Smith and William Copeland Borlase, fellow-naturalists, and J.O. Halliwell, son-in-law of the famous book-collector Sir Thomas Phillips, who engaged J.T.B. as his assistant and illustrator.

Starting with minor notes in Cornish periodicals, J.T.B. became during the 1860s a prolific contributor to the journals of learned bodies. Most of his work covers what we would now regard as standing monuments and conventional field-archaeology, and in 1866 he was elected a Fellow of the Society of Antiquaries. His name became familiar far outside Cornish circles. Actual books headed the output: *Ancient Crosses and Other Antiquities in the West of Cornwall* (1857), the companion *East Cornwall* in 1858, *A Week*

J.T. Blight, circa 1864.

at the Land's End in 1861, and – published by Parker of Oxford, a most desirable cachet to obtain – his *Churches of West Cornwall*, etc., in 1865. Most of these went into second and third 'editions', actually re-issues.

Success, seemingly apparent to us on paper, only spelled out failure to poor J.T.B. He made very little real income; he was an economic prisoner at Morrab Place, Penzance, of his admittedly loving family; and he was precluded by birth, distance, poverty and lack of sufficient acquaintances from participating in the glittering world of London literati and the supposedly endless procession of antiquarian meetings or *conversazioni*. The sad course of the 1860s has now been delineated, with sympathy and skill, by John Michell in his *A Short Life at the Land's End* (privately, Bath, 1977). To frustration and intemperateness of character was added a third element. A clinical psychiatrist might be able to offer more precise diagnoses, but in short J.T.B. was overtaken by madness. Paranoia, a form of persecution mania, an increasing withdrawal from reality and reported violence all led to his committal in 1871 to the County Asylum at Bodmin. By 1883, there was insufficient money to maintain him as a private patient; William Bolitho and other well-wishers in Penzance raised a 'Blight fund' to buy the necessary annuity. As John Michell has explained, Parker of Oxford (re-issuing *Churches of West Cornwall* in October 1884) noted, erroneously, the author's recent death. This fiction was upheld even by those who knew that J.T.B. lingered at Bodmin, and his real death was 23 January 1911. During the long decades in the 'private side', was there any relief? We know that William Iago, FSA, Chaplain to the Asylum and a good as well as a learned man, befriended his unhappy fellow antiquary, and there is a mysterious photograph around 1900 – it shows a party visiting the Harlyn Bay, Iron Age cemetery, excavations – where a recognisable Reverend W. Iago partly conceals a dejected, bearded figure with downcast head ...

But *A Week at the Land's End* takes us fairly and squarely to J.T.B.'s happier period, if truly happy he could be.

And a recent discovery of a carte-de-visite photograph (re-produced on page v above) depicts the author as we would prefer to remember him. Publishing it in 1988, I suggested that it was made about 1864, at Penzance by J.T.B.'s friend Robert Preston, *doyen* of early Cornish photographers, so that the subject could have a stock to send out to friends and admirers (including R.S. Hawker of Morwenstow, who happened to be Preston's uncle). This is the man who wrote *Land's End*, completing it as a labour of love on May-Day of 1861 and, in the manner of a young romantic with enough authority to pontificate, could state: 'Where, again, in our native land, shall we find a tract of equal extent off-ering so many attractions in the marvellous variety and grandeur of its scenery, the deep interest of its historical associations, and the vast abundance of its ancient monu-ments?' J.T.B. wrote, here, with conviction; a prescient view of the richness of the Land's End peninsula's (and the Lizard's) wealth of archaeological sites that in 1862 led him to produce his pioneering pamphlet, *List of Antiquities in the Hundreds of Kirrier and Penwith*.

What gives *A Week at the Land's End*, still, its particular charm? Partly of course the author's illustrations and the way in which they complement his text; the minute detail of the background (cf. 'Boscawen-Un Circle' or 'Buryas Bridge') as well as the style recalls Tenniel's interpretation of *Alice*. There have been many other descriptions of the Land's End, and J.T.B.'s was not the first; but it strikes me as having been the first, and perhaps the best, to assume a reader who was simply prepared to go for a long ramble – as J.T.B. so often did with his father Robert or brother Joseph – and look at *everything*. My own copy of the original edition bears the bookplate of Prescott Row, founder of the Homeland Handbooks, to whom this work must have had the same appeal that it has held for countless readers since 1861.

Blight's other contribution to the archive of his native Cornwall was, and remains, his accuracy. *Land's End* is a general work and its details are elaborated, professionally, in his articles and their differing, sometimes measured, depictions. J.T.B. saw, noted, drew, paced, ruled and recorded. Not all the antiquities exist today; many of west Cornwall's churches, as J.T.B. knew them, had yet to suffer late Victorian refurbishment. With the reams of unpublished drawings and sketches, J.T.B.'s published output makes up a personal monument, standing conveniently between the great eighteenth-century volumes of Dr William Borlase and the near-total record professionally compiled in the last thirty years of our own century. For this, let alone for the simple pleasure of his text and his enthusiasm, our gratitude to John Thomas Blight remains as strong as ever. The sadness of the years from 1871 to 1911 cannot be swept away, but it is the younger Blight, the enchanted rambler from Penzance with his pencil, his vasculum and his obvious indifference to such trivia as meals and the time of return to Morrab Place, that we would prefer to know. *A Week at the Land's End* allows us, once again, to know him very well indeed.

CHARLES THOMAS

Institute of Cornish Studies
1989

PREFACE.

———◆———

The following pages are intended to illustrate, by aid of pen and pencil, the extreme western point of England; its romantic scenery, its natural productions, and its ancient legends.

Many who have not visited the spot attach to it only the peculiar interest of its being that part of our native land which stretches farthest into the great Atlantic. The Author has attempted to show that the district has something more to recommend it to notice than the mere charm of its name—"The Land's End."

J. T. B.

Penzance: May 1, 1861.

CONTENTS.

———◆———

CHAPTER I.

CHAPTER II.

CONTENTS.

CHAPTER III.

CHAPTER IV.

CHAPTER V.

CONTENTS.

LIST OF ILLUSTRATIONS

(DRAWN AND ENGRAVED BY THE AUTHOR).

ILLUSTRATIONS (AS SEPARATE PLATES).

ILLUSTRATIONS IN THE TEXT.

LIST OF ILLUSTRATIONS.

LIST OF ILLUSTRATIONS.

NEWLYN.

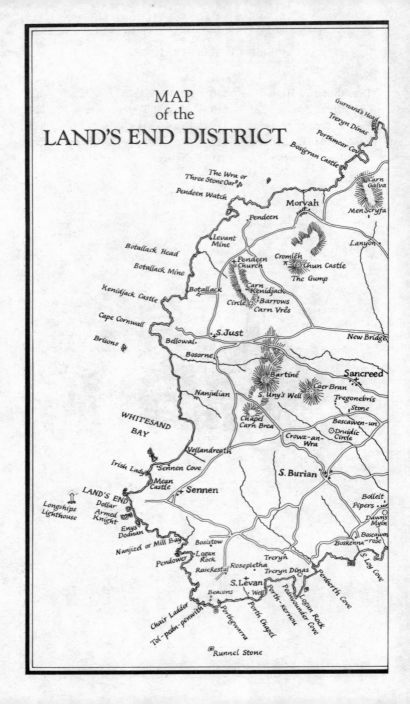

MAP
of the
LAND'S END DISTRICT

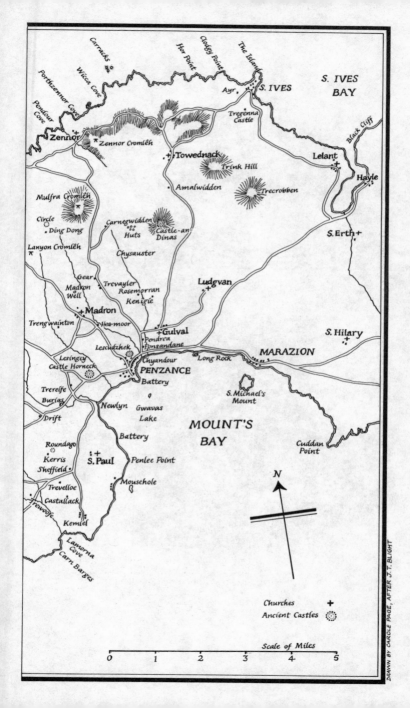

DRAWN BY CAROLE PAGE, AFTER J. T. BLIGHT

THE LAND'S END.

A WEEK AT THE LAND'S END.

CHAPTER I.

THE region of the West of England presents us with
scenes and memories which no other district of our
land affords.   There are the bold, magnificent cliffs,
and

      " Towering headlands crown'd with mist,"

guardians of the western coast.   There are hoary
monuments of ages past — many of them well preserved from the destroying hands of Time, yet surrounded by a deep halo of mystery, which the
speculations of the antiquary can scarcely penetrate.

In early days, it is said, the rich merchants of
Phœnicia made long voyages hither, and in exchange for a few trinkets procured the valuable
metals of the soil. The Roman eagles here contested
with the warlike Cornish; and the sea-kings, the
piratical Danes, made fell swoops wherever they
could effect a landing on the coast. It was here, too,
that the Saxons overthrew the army of Howel, the
last of the Cornish kings. Besides kings, princes,
warriors, and merchants, with all the train of romantic associations connected with them, shadows
of a deeper kind pass before us, in the shape of long-
robed Druids, the priests of Celtic days,— here they
had their altars on the high hills and cairns, here

" True to the awful rites of old,"

they " paced the vast circle's solemn round." Inscriptions and records they have left none, for the
deeds of this age were remembered through the
unwritten utterances of the Bard, and thus was
handed down the traditionary lore of a spot once
occupied by men whose religion and practices have
for ever vanished away,—the rough unhewn stone is
the only visible landmark of the peculiarities of their
faith and worship.

The inhabitants were in a state of civilisation
when other portions of the island might be deemed
a " land unknown." Diodorus Siculus says, " The
natives of that part of Britain, which is called
Belerium, (*i. e.* the Land's End district), are not
only very hospitable, but also are civilised in their

living, through the intercourse which they have kept up with the merchants of foreign countries."

Here the Christian religion dawned on England. Long before the preaching of St. Augustine and his monks, the Cornish Britons had a church of their own; and ancient symbols of their faith — marking the triumph of the Cross over the dark superstition which preceded its introduction — may still be seen on the moor and by the wayside. Irish saints and pilgrims wandered over this ground, erecting cells and giving names to churches and holy stations.

Where, again, in our native land, shall we find a tract of equal extent offering so many attractions in the marvellous variety and grandeur of its scenery, the deep interest of its historical associations, and the vast abundance of its ancient monuments?

The remains of castles and fortifications which crown the summits of the most important hills and border the coast, standing on the very edges of the cliffs, are evidences of the fierce warfare once carried on: indeed, no portion of the whole country of the same area retains more numerous vestiges of the structures which our forefathers reared to protect themselves from their several foes.

The antiquities of the district, however, form but one of its chief features. The character of the coast is particularly favourable for the study of the geologist, presenting, as it does, in the natural section of cliffs, the exact structure and relations of the rocks of which the country is composed. As we advance we shall find how fertile are the hills and valleys to

the botanist—the sea and its shores to the naturalist.
The mildness of the climate attracts rare birds for
the gratification of the ornithologist —whilst the
artist may have ample subjects to engage his pencil
for a lifetime.

Although most of the tract is granite, patches of
the slate formation appear here and there along the
coast, on the western side at considerable intervals
only, but on the east it is more continuous. The
Land's End district presents the finest, we might
almost say the only, granite cliffs in England, and
formed of the most enduring materials receive the
first onset of the Atlantic.

The northern part is bleak and barren; with a few
exceptions such is the character of the whole length
of the north coast of Cornwall. The south and much
of the interior present more cheerful aspects, many
spots being cultivated to the water's edge. Although
in general appearance the country is open and exposed, yet are there many beautiful sheltered nooks
and valleys, watered by rivulets which trickle from
the heath-clad hills and rocky cairns, blending with
the sea over the white sand of some pretty cove, or
dashing headlong from the rugged cliffs.

The principal mining field in the neighbourhood
is the parish of St. Just. Those who are not familiar
with scenes connected with the search for the mineral
productions of the earth, would be surprised to wit-
ness the fearful labours of the miner.

Fishing also affords employment to a number of
the inhabitants, and in the little creeks and coves

around the coast the fishing boats, when not in use, are drawn high above the tide, and securely fastened. Old crab-pots, nets, ropes, masts, and pieces of wreck lie scattered about in picturesque confusion, whilst the fisherman's cot 'may be seen bordering the very wave, or in some sheltered glen hard by. The sketcher might fill many pages of his book in such localities as these.

Although a large proportion of the land is uncultivated, yet portions of the district have long been remarkable for their fertility and productiveness, the London markets being largely supplied with early vegetables by the gardeners; and many of the farms situated on the decomposed granite exhibit crops of corn equal to those grown in the best lands of England.

Walking through the fields during the close of harvest, a stranger might be surprised to hear loud shouts, and see the reapers waving their hands, whilst one holds up a handful of wheat; this is the last handful cut, which finishes the harvest. This is called "cutting the neck," a very ancient custom. In days of old the neck was interwoven with flowers, and dedicated to the goddess of harvest. A pleasing memory this, of ancient times, and one which shows that our forefathers — if they did not worship aright — yet testified their gratitude for being permitted to gather safely the "kindly fruits of the earth." It is questionable if those who still observe the ceremony know for what reason they do so; as with many other good old customs bequeathed us, the forms are adhered to, but their meaning is lost and forgotten. Another harvest custom peculiar to the district, or rather to Cornwall, is the erection of the *arish* or *windmows*. These are formed by sheaves built up in the fields into regular solid cones, about twelve feet high, the heads of the stalks turned inward; the top is capped by a sheaf of reed or corn inverted. This custom is probably owing to the uncertainty and moisture of the weather, some such mode of treatment being found necessary to protect the corn from rain and wind; it remains in this state for several days, and sometimes weeks, before it is carried away. This is done nowhere else in England, except at the western extremities of Devonshire. Other curious practices which still remain, shadows of a past age, will be noticed as we proceed through this " fabled land of giants."

The surface of the country must have worn a very different aspect at one time from what it now does. There is no doubt that it was more densely wooded, remains of ancient forests having been discovered at various places; that this was the case is also evident from the old Cornish names. The oak and the hazel appear to have been particularly plentiful, affording thick coverts for the wolf * and the deer, with other wild animals, which once abounded throughout England. But centuries have gone by, and Time in his

---

* The late Mr. Davies Gilbert has more than once asserted that the last native wolf seen in England was captured at Rospeith in Ludgvan.

PENZANCE.

course has wrought vast changes on the country and the manners of its people.

Almost all the names are in ancient Cornish; thus, the chief town of the district, Penzance ("Pensantia" of Ray and Willoughby), *Pen-sans,* the "Holy-headland," seems to have been so called on account of a chapel, dedicated to St. Anthony, the patron of fishermen, which once stood on a projecting point near the present quay. In the chapel-yard of St. Mary's is the fragment of an old cross supposed to have belonged to this chapel.

The situation of the town is one of peculiar beauty, sloping down from an elevation of about one hundred feet to the edge of the sea, where it terminates in a fine promenade about half a mile in length, with the wide expanse of the bay spread before it. A stroll along the beach, which, subject to the influence of the east and south-west winds, is now of sand, now of pebbles—is a delightful one. After a rough sea large quantities of sea-weed are thrown up, when the most delicate specimens may be gathered. Very beautiful are they when pressed on smooth sheets of paper, in the folio of the amateur; but how different they look in their native element, to watch them waving to and fro with the motion of the waves, to peer down into the great gloomy recesses, where are blended dark masses of green, and crimson, and purple, forming arcades and dense groves, and long vistas stretching away into the mysterious shades of the deep. "Around the huge rocks the perennial fringes of olive fuci undulate in graceful folds among

the swelling waves, and the tall tangle bows its pliant
stem as—

> " ' The ocean old,—
>   Centuries old,—
>   Strong as youth, and as uncontrolled,
>   Paces restless to and fro,
>   Up and down the sands of gold.' "

" For ages," says the writer just quoted, " have the
weeds of the sea been heedlessly disregarded or
despised. The vilest epithet the polished Roman
knew was, *algâ projectâ vilior*. Horace too, wrote
alga inutilis; and there may be many yet to ex-
claim with the Scotch professor of the last century,
' Pooh, pooh, sir! only a bundle of sea-weeds!' But
when the Apostle Peter slept at the house of Simon
the tanner, he dreamt a great dream; a dream memorable to the end of time—a dream that was a
waking truth to be set in golden letters, and engraven
on the hearts of rich and poor, wise and unwise.
' There is nothing common nor unclean.' " * This
weed is used for other purposes than filling folios or
decorating aquariums; large quantities are collected
by agriculturists, as manure for the land. When it
is washing in, men go into the surf and with long
rakes drag it beyond the reach of the tide. When it
cannot be had in this manner, they proceed with
boats to the rocks and pare it off with scythes affixed
to long poles.

Amongst other rare fish which have been captured
in Mount's Bay, may be mentioned the torpedo, or
electric ray, taken several years following in a trawl,

* "Art-Journal," 1858.

the mailed gurnard, and the long-finned tunny (*Thynnus alalonga*), of which an engraving is here introduced.

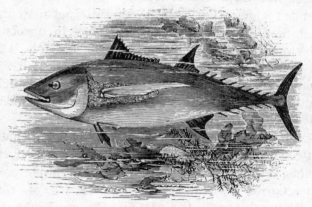

THE LONG-FINNED TUNNY.

There is sufficient evidence to prove, in the remains which still exist, that trees once grew where the sea now washes on this beach. Near the Lariggan rocks, on which a mine was formerly worked, we find, by digging a little into the stratum of sand, a black vegetable mould, full of woodland detritus, such as the branches, leaves, and nuts of coppice wood, together with the carbonised roots and trunks of forest trees of large growth. All these are manifestly indigenous; and, from the freshness and preservation of some of the remains, the inundation of sand and water must have been sudden and simultaneous; and the circumstance of ripe nuts and leaves remaining together, shows that the irruption

happened in the autumn or the beginning of winter.
This vegetable substratum has been traced seaward
as far as the ebb permits, and is found continuous
and of like nature.* A forest is supposed to have
extended along the coast to St. Michael's Mount,
which was described as "a hoare rock in a wood,"
and stood five or six miles from the sea; the bay
was said to have been a plain of five or six miles in
extent, formed into parishes, each having its church,
and laid out in meadows, corn-fields, and woods.
This account is regarded as a monkish fable.

As it is now generally considered beyond dispute,
that St. Michael's Mount is the "Ictis" of Diodorus
Siculus, it is evident that no change of importance
has occurred in the natural appearance of that
singular rock for the last eighteen hundred years at
least. An inundation of some sort certainly happened at a remote period, but of this we have no
correct account.

Penzance has been very much improved within
the last few years, and from its natural qualifications
might be made one of the first watering-places in
the kingdom. Associated with this town is the name
of Pellew, Lord Exmouth; it was also the birth-
place of Sir Humphry Davy, whose name will ever
be revered as a philosopher whose wonderful scientific
researches and discoveries were employed, not for
his own glory, but for the welfare of his fellow-
creatures. In this his native place it might be
thought that many "memories" and anecdotes re-

* See Trans. Geological Society of Cornwall, vol. ii.

lating to so great a man would be retained, such, however, is not the case.

Near the eastern entrance to the town is the site of one of the ancient castles which are to be met with so frequently in this district. The place is still called Lesgudzhek, the " castle of the bloody field." Some consider the termination of the word a corruption of Caradoc, who was a king of Cornwall about A.D. 360; thus it would be the *Court of Caradoc.* From this mound we have almost a bird's-eye view of the town; the bay is also seen to great advantage.

By using the word " castle," one unacquainted with Cornish antiquities might picture to himself a fine old structure, of battlements and loopholes, massive crumbling walls overspread with ivy, in which some haughty lord resided in feudal times, holding sway over his surrounding territory. But the remains with which we have to do were constructed ages before the " memory of man."

What are here known as castles are merely rude entrenchments and embankments, the largest perhaps not more than ten or twelve feet high, and formed with loose stones and earth, no cement being used. There was another of these fortifications about a quarter of a mile west of the town, at Castle Horneck, the *Iron-Castle,* now the seat of S. Borlase, Esq., representative of the ancient Cornish family of that name—of which the celebrated antiquary was a distinguished member. On the top of the hill, which rises behind this delightful residence, some remains of the old embankments may still be seen, enclosing

about an acre and a half, now planted with fir trees :
it is known by the name of Lezingey Round. This,
however, must not be confounded with Castle Horneck,
which is thought to have been so denominated from
its supposed strength, and was built by the ancient
baronial family of the Tyers, who were lords of this
district early in the times of the Plantagenets.

Penzance is in the parish of Madron, but was, as far
back as the year 1680, constituted a separate chapelry.
There are several pathways through lawns and green
fields leading to Madron Church, which stands on a
commanding elevation. It is truly a splendid prospect
of sea and land from this spot. On the eastern side
of the noble bay which is spread out before us is seen
the land which terminates with the Lizard Point;
near the northern shore stands St. Michael's Mount,
now perhaps connected by a narrow causeway to the
mainland, but ere the sun sets it will be an island;
in the middle distance and foreground are fertile
valleys, slopes, and rounded hills, rich and beautiful
beyond description.

Madron Church is not without interest to the
archæologist—the east end is remarkable; it is the
genuine east end of the original early English church
of about 1260 or 1270. A modern window has sup-
planted probably an unequal triplet of laurets. This
accounts for the fact that the nave and chancel are so
narrow. The church was enlarged in the fifteenth
century. It then consisted of a narrow nave and chancel, the walls of which were pierced with arcades, and
wide aisles added, north and south. The admirable

sedile and piscina are worthy of notice. There are several mural monuments recording the virtues of members of old families in the neighbourhood. No carvings of interest will be found, excepting perhaps that on the outside of the pew belonging to the Trengwainton estate ; it represents the arms of Henry VIII., France and England quarterly, surrounded with the garter and ensigned with a large crown. Supporters, Red Dragon for Cadwallader, last king of the Britons, from whom he claimed descent. On the left a greyhound, argent, collared gules, for Somerset. Badges, the Portcullis (placed below) from his mother of the family of Beaufort; and the white and red rose (York and Lancaster united).

An old tomb here has the following quaint inscription—

> " Belgium me birth, Britaine me breeding gave,
> Cornwall a wife, ten children and a grave."

This church is said to have been bestowed on the Knights Templars by Henry Pomeroy. At Landithy immediately adjoining was the college or preceptory of the Templars ; some of the rooms were adorned with curious portraits of English kings and queens. This building has been taken down within the last few years, and a farm-house erected on its site.

Proceeding in a northerly direction from Madron village—or in Cornish phrase, " church-town "—through some pathway fields until we arrive at a clump of fir trees, we turn down by a gateway on the right through marshy ground. Here was a baptistery, the four walls of which are still standing. The doorway remains on the south side, and within are, the well, the *mensa* of the altar, and the step by which the sacrarium was raised above the little nave. The altar is remarkable for a mortice sunk in its centre, and intended apparently to receive an image of the saint. It is not very clear who St. Madron was. Some speak of one Madan a British king in these parts, before Julius Cæsar landed in Britain, who lived and died here, and in memory of whom this parish is now called Madran or Madron. St. Madron is regarded by others as a female, said to have been buried at Minster Church in this county. In the entries of the taxation of Pope Nicholas, A.D. 1291, Madron is called " Ecclesia Sancti Maderni" which contradicts the former legend. St. Madron's Well was reduced to its present ruinous condition by Shrubsall, governor of Pendennis Castle, during Cromwell's usurpation ; we shall trace other marks of his destroying hands as we progress. The spring was resorted to as a test of faith —

> " Plunge thy right hand in S. Madron's spring !
> If true to its troth be the palm you bring ;
> But if a false sigil thy fingers bear,
> Lay them the rather on the burning share."

The water was also supposed to possess miraculous virtues, and some persons at the present time believe in its efficacy. On this subject and of this well I have given a more particular account in a previous work, " Ancient Crosses &c. of Cornwall."

Before leaving the spot let us look about and

notice some of the beautiful " weeds " which grow in damp and boggy places such as this. Trailing over the mossy stones by the rivulet of " holy water " is the Cornish moneywort, *Sibthorpia Europæa*. The

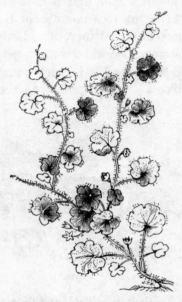

CORNISH MONEYWORT (*Sibthorpia Europæa*).

mildness of the climate permits it to flourish all the year round, whilst, if planted in the most sheltered spots in the midland counties, it sighs for its native soil and withers away. It is elsewhere in England a rare plant. Cornwall is well known to botanists as being remarkably rich in the smaller flowering plants which thrive in wet places.

On the right hand side of the road, a few yards

beyond the gateway through which we passed to go
to the Well, is an old cross, now broken in two—it
served originally to guide the pilgrim and devotee to
the baptistery.

A walk of about a mile and a half on the road to
Morvah will bring us to a monument belonging to a
very early period of our history. The Lanyon Cromlêh
has a strange appearance when we first get sight of it—
standing on high ground it is very conspicuous, and
looks not unlike a great tripod.   As the Cromlêh is

LANYON CROMLÊH.

found in the countries once inhabited by the Celts,
its use is supposed to have originated with that race.
The Druids used similar monuments, but they were
not exclusively confined to them, as they have been
found where the Druids never had footing.   Similar
monuments appear to have been worshipped in
Ireland, and Dr. Borlase refers to one in Wales on
which crosses were cut.   As it is well known that the
early Christians so marked the blocks of stone held
sacred by the heathen, that when they knelt to

them they might pay a kind of justifiable adoration, it seems probable that some of them were regarded as objects of worship. Some have considered them Druid altars on which sacred fires were kindled, but any one who has seen them will soon dismiss this conjecture, as from their construction they are not applicable to this purpose. They were probably tombs, raised in honour of distinguished personages. Some are formed as *kist-vaens,* i. e. chests made ot stone—this one could never have been so constructed. Dr. Borlase dug beneath it, and found that a pit had been made there, but he discovered no remains of any consequence. The doctor describes this monument as high enough for a man to sit on horseback under it, a feat now impossible, for the height from the ground to the cover stone is only five feet; the difference between its elevation now and when seen by Dr. Borlase can only be accounted for on the supposition that the supporters were by some means shortened when the top-stone was replaced in 1824 ; in 1816 it was thrown down during a violent storm, and restored to its original position by use of the powerful machinery brought into the county to raise the celebrated Logan Rock. A few yards south of the cromlêh are the remains of a small barrow ; which if opened might, perhaps, repay the curious for investigation. The cap-stone of the cromlêh is eighteen and a half feet long and measures at the broadest part nine feet: its form is irregular — the average thickness is about a foot and a half. It is vain to

speculate on the means first employed to raise such
a ponderous mass, and

> " the heart,
> Aching with thoughts of human littleness,
> Asks, without hope or knowing, whose the strength
> That poised thee here."

It has been beaten by the storms of ages —

> " The naked Briton here has paused to gaze —
> Ere bells were chimed,
> Or the thronged hamlet smoked with social fires."

In the middle of a field about half a mile distant
is another cromlêh overthrown. A skull and other
human bones were found beneath it. Ancient remains
were formerly very superstitiously regarded; and it
is to be regretted that this kind of respect for them
amongst the ignorant is dying out, as it preserved
many from destruction. The person who pulled
down this cromlêh is said to have brought a number
of misfortunes about him in consequence; thus his
cattle died and crops failed, which left a warning impression on the minds of his neighbours.

The word cromlêh, means a *crooked flat stone.*
Lêh, Cornish, *lech,* Welsh, a flat stone; *crom,* crooked.
Lanyon, the name of the estate, does not appear to
be a Cornish word, though it has been read as such,
the interpretation being "the furzy enclosure." *Lan*
is Cornish for enclosure and also for church; there
was an ancient chapel here dedicated to St. Bridget.
It is, however, most probably a French word. There
are still in the country descendants of the ancient

family of that name, and the popular tradition is
that they were derived from two brothers who came
over from France with Isabel, consort of Richard II.,
and gave their names to the bartons on which they
fixed their residences; it is said in confirmation that
their arms were the same as those of the town of
Lanion in Brittany.

Beyond Lanyon village, in a furzy thicket, called
in Cornwall a "croft" on the right hand side of the
road is another curious monument, here illustrated.
This is the Mên-an-tol, "holed stone," through which

THE MÊN-AN-TOL.

the country people drew their children to cure them
of pains in the back. It is supposed to have been
originally used for some Druidical ceremonies.

The Mên-Scryfa, "written-stone," is now within
half a mile. As an ancient inscribed monument, it
is one of the most important in the kingdom.
The inscription is, "Rialobran-Cunoval Fil"; at
length, "Rialobranus Cunovali Filius," signifying
that Rialobran, the son of Cunoval, was buried here.

It has never been ascertained who this Rialobran was. Rioval, a British leader who lived in the year 454, and Rivallo (alias Rywathon) brother of Harold, the son of Earl Godwin, have been hinted at. The question is not now likely to be settled; and in a few years, most probably, the stone itself will be numbered amongst the things that were. A clown of the neighbourhood, possessed with a longing desire to become suddenly rich, had heard that crocks of gold were occasionally found buried beneath great stones; the thought haunted him day and night; and no peace had he until he relieved his mind by digging a deep pit around the Mên-Scryfa, and causing it to fall, face downward, in which disgraceful position it has ever since remained. The inscription was written before the alphabet was corrupted, i. e. before the letters were joined together by unnatural links, and the down strokes of one made to serve for two; which corruptions crept into the Roman alphabet, used by the Cornish Britons, and increased more and more until the Saxon letters came into use, about the time of Athelstan's conquest. The most observable deviation from the Roman orthography in this monument is, that the cross stroke of the Roman N is not diagonal as it should be, nor yet quite horizontal as used in the sixth century; it is therefore probable that this inscription was made before the middle of the sixth century. Though some have considered it a heathen monument, Dr. Borlase thought it Christian, and erected before it became usual to place the cross before the name.

A popular tradition is, that a great battle was fought near the spot; that one of the chiefs or leaders was slain and buried here; that this inscribed granite pillar was erected to mark the place of burial; and that its length, about nine feet, was the exact height of the warrior.

A rugged road leads hence in a northerly direction : after following it for two or three hundred yards, we shall observe on the common a large flat stone with a cross cut on it, so marked to show that four parishes, Madron, Gulval, Morvah, and Zennor, meet at this point. According to a legend, some Saxon Kings used it as a dining-table, but another rock, near the Land's End, claims the honour, and it is evident that it has the greatest right to it,—the arguments in its favour are certainly more reasonable. Cairn Galva, a bold and curious pile of granite rock, about 623 feet above the level of the sea, is a conspicuous object from this locality. With the golden furze, purple heath, whortleberry, and the bright mosses and lichens on the rocks, this cairn has in colour a gorgeous appearance. There are beautiful green patches of turf here and there, soft and smooth as velvet. Near the summit of the most westerly crag of the range is a logan stone, easily got at and easily moved; it looks as if it had been detached from the main rock—and a mass of cubical blocks at the base, almost as regular in form as if artificially wrought, appear as if they had been violently and suddenly thrown from a more elevated position, by some terrible convulsion.

The botanist may find here *Polypodium Phegopteris, Hymenophyllum Wilsoni,* and *H. Tunbridgense* and *Sticta crocata.*

On high ground, about a mile south-east of the rock marking the conjunction of the four parishes, is Ding Dong, one of the oldest mines in the county, and said to have been worked by the Jews, who at one period were engaged in managing the mines in Cornwall. The tradition is strongly held in this western part, and when the tinners discover the remains of an old smelting-place for tin they always call it a "Jew's house." Old blocks of tin, too, are occasionally found of a peculiar form,—these are named "Jews' pieces;" and the stream works of tin, that have been deserted by the labourers, are considered "Jews' works," styled in Cornish "Attal Sarasin," or the "leavings of the Saracens," as the Jews were denominated. The names of some places in the west of Cornwall appear also to support the idea that the Jews had some connection with them. Near Ding Dong are two ancient barrows and the remains of a Druidic circle, popularly called the "Nine Maidens."

Even on this barren spot are to be found plants worth noticing, especially *Littorella lacustris.*

Had a southerly course been taken from the Mên-Scryfa we should have crossed the Morvah road, and following a track, rugged and worn like the bed of a torrent, should soon have reached the summit of the hill on which is Castle Chûn. Approaching the hill on the north side, may be seen the remains of ancient

British huts, called by the people the "Crellas."
They are circular in form and of various sizes, the
largest about forty feet in diameter; there are no
remains of roofs and the entrances are very narrow.
They are built without the use of cement or mortar,
and show some skill in their construction. Fragments of pottery have been found within them.
Overgrown with furze and brambles, they now have
a dreary appearance. A road, of the same period as
the huts, partly excavated out of the soil, and guarded
on either side by large stones, communicates with
the castle. The accompanying plan will give an idea

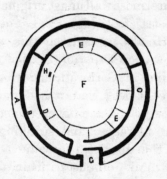

PLAN OF CHÛN CASTLE.

of the construction of this fortification. A is a ditch,
B, a wall about five feet thick; then another ditch or
fosse C, thirty feet wide. The wall D is three feet
wide at the top, expands at the base; next this wall
are several lodgements EE of unequal length, but
all of the same breadth—thirty feet; these are
imagined to have been constructed for shelter in

rough weather. The area F, within the works, is 125 feet from east to west, 110 from north to south; the entrance G, called the "iron gateway," is guarded by walls crossing the ditches, and faces W.S.W. The principal fosse has four traverses, including the two at the entrance. At H is a well with steps to go down to the water. This plan is from Dr. Borlase's, the castle being more perfect in his time, therefore it is of greater value than any which might now be made on the spot, as the old walls have been very seriously injured, large quantities of the stone having been carried away for building purposes. Dr. Borlase thought the outermost wall must originally have been not less than ten feet high, the innermost about fifteen feet. He also considered this castle to show a military knowledge superior to that of any other work of the kind in Cornwall, and that it was constructed by the Danes; that it had only temporary shelters, because the Danes accustomed to a colder climate wanted no more; and speaking generally of the castles of the district, the same authority says, "these castles have no houses within them, as most probably they would have had, if erected by and for the natives, but only some low huts for soldiers." The doctor was strongly possessed with this idea of the Danes; but may not the ruined huts we have seen connected to the castle by a road, be the works of the natives of the country, constructed near the castle for protection? and it appears evident that they gave name to the castle itself—the word "Chûn" or "Choone" signifying a "dwelling on a common."

We shall by and by meet with another supposed ancient British village, more important than this, also very near an old fortification. There are remains of seven hill castles between St. Michael's Mount and the Land's End, from which signals might be made from one to another. This part of Cornwall appears to have been the last stronghold of the Britons. Driven before foreign invaders, they retreated amongst the wild hills and cairns of Bolerium, and reared these fortifications in their last efforts to maintain their freedom. Surely there is more reason for supposing them the works of the inhabitants than of strangers.

On the declivity of the hill and on the plain beneath Chûn Castle are scores of small barrows, heaps of stones, piled about the height of three feet : some have been opened ; no urns or bones were found, but the earth was discoloured as if it had been subjected to fire. They lie scattered about in all directions, as if there had been some fierce battle here, and the dead had been burnt and their ashes buried on the spot where they had fallen. On the summit of the hill a short distance south-west of the castle is a fine cromlêh, the cap-stone nearly thirteen feet long and eleven and a half wide, its elevation about four feet. A barrow of stones formerly surrounded it, of which very little is now to be seen. The castle is in the parish of Madron, but the cromlêh, though but a few hundred yards from it, stands on the border of the parishes of St. Just and Morvah.

In returning to Penzance we so manage our route

as to pass by Trengwainton Cairn, a romantic spot,
well deserving a visit.   On this cairn is an ancient
cross.   *Lecanora milvina*, a rare lichen, is found here,
and at many other places in the neighbourhood.
Crossing the belt of trees near Trengwainton Cairn,
the rhododendron may be seen growing almost wild,
in great luxuriance.   A beautiful clear stream runs
through the valley beneath, in its course filling three

CLUB MOSS (*Lycopodium inundatum*).

ponds whose banks are crowded with thick coppice,
of which the laurel forms a large portion.   If in a
botanical mood one need not be idle in this valley.
In a boggy spot below the last pond, grows a plant
of some rarity, *Lycopodium inundatum*.   It is of a
beautiful refreshing green hue, and spreads thickly
over the ground, shooting up now and then its
flowering stalks, which are from two to three inches

high. This is its only habitat in the district. Most persons know how sacred the mistletoe was to the Druids; but there were other plants which they held in high esteem; the fir club-moss, another species of this genus, was one, and was gathered with much ceremony. It was not to be touched or cut with iron, which was considered too base a metal, nor was the bare hand thought worthy of that honour, but a peculiar vesture or sagus applied by means of the right hand; the vesture must have been holy and taken off from some sacred person privately and with the left hand only. The gatherer was to have his feet naked, being previously washed in pure water, and he was to be clothed in a white garment. He was to offer a sacrifice of bread and wine before proceeding to gather it, and it was to be carried from the place of its nativity in a clean new napkin. It was preserved as a charm against all misfortunes, and the fumigation of it was thought good against all defects of the eyes.

It has been thought advisable in this sketch of the Land's End district to pay some attention to what is now an object of very general interest, namely, the Natural History of the country. The western part of Cornwall has long been known to be rich in botanical and zoological productions; but as so many objects of importance have to be noticed, a work of this kind will not admit of copious detail in every branch, yet enough of the rarer and more interesting features in the different departments of natural science will be mentioned to give at least a fair

estimate of what the district can show. The Land's
End peninsula has been long celebrated for its
peculiarly mild temperature, which, with a large
share of humidity, renders it a rich and fertile tract
for the botanist. There will be found scattered
throughout these pages occasional illustrations of rare
or peculiar plants. It will, of course, be understood
that they are not always confined solely to the spot
at which they may happen to be placed; two or
three I have introduced merely for some local or
historical interest attached to them: in the selection of the others and in the botanical notes relating
to the district, I have been directed and assisted by
Mr. J. Ralfs. As to the value of these notes it will
be unnecessary to make any comment, as Mr. Ralfs'
name is familiar to every student of botany.

With regard to fish, the Cornish coast has afforded,
through the powerful agency of the Messrs. Couch,
ample means for the compilation, by the late Mr.
Yarrell, of the best and most complete work on
" British Fishes " extant. I have much pleasure in
acknowledging my obligations to Mr. R. Q. Couch for
valuable aid in this department.

A very considerable portion of all the known British species of birds, both land and aquatic, which
have been referred to by Mr. Yarrell, in his work on
" British Birds," have been found in the neighbourhood of Penzance. Many of them are preserved in
the museum at Penzance ; and two private collections
in the town, together, contain almost a complete
museum of British birds captured in the district,

including the Scilly Isles. In glancing at the different parishes, illustrations will be given of rare specimens procured from those localities; these have been made from the valuable collection in the possession of Mr. E. H. Rodd, of Penzance, who has kindly supplied the ornithological information diffused throughout this volume.

To the numerous interesting birds of the district which will be found mentioned, the following rare species may be added:—Honey buzzard; scops-

RICHARD'S PIPIT.

eared owl and long-eared owl; great grey shrike, redback shrike and woodchat shrike; grasshopper warbler, fire-crested wren, lesser whitethroat, black redstart, great spotted woodpecker and wryneck, the latter only during migration; brambling finch, siskin finch; ortolan bunting, snow bunting; white-winged crossbill, tree sparrow, hawfinch; grey-headed, yellow, and continental white-wagtails; short-toed lark, crested lark, Richard's pipit, tree pipit; sand martin; white-bellied swift; turtle-dove, waxwing, bee-eater. The following water birds will complete the list: — Sabines, little and ivory gulls; pomarrhine skua; Arctic and lesser terns; the great snipe and the brown longbeak; the redshank sandpiper; the little, Temminck's, American, Schinz's and buff-breasted stints; Kentish plover; night heron and spoonbill; great northern, red-throated, and black-throated divers; grey and red phalaropes; storm, fork-tailed, and great petrels; Arctic and lesser terns; goosander and redbreasted merganser; white-fronted, bean, brent, and bernicle geese.

In visiting any district or country, it always affords great pleasure, as well as instruction, to notice the objects of nature which in some form or other are ever presenting themselves before us; to examine the beautiful flowers, and the brilliantly coloured and minute insects, which are hovering and alighting around on every side; to watch and listen to the "feathered choristers" of the woods as they fly from branch to branch; to know their wondrous forms, to remember the associations connected with them, and what has been pleasantly told of them. There is a beautiful legend relating to the crossbill; the soft downy feathers of this bird are steeped in crimson; and as its name implies, the bill is crossed, the lower mandible projecting on one side beyond the upper part. The story, rendered familiar by Longfellow's translation, is that when our Lord was on the cross, this bird endeavoured to release Him.

" At the ruthless nail of iron,
   A poor bird is striving there.

" Stained with blood, and never tiring,
   With its beak it doth not cease,
From the cross 'twould free the Saviour,
   Its Creator's Son release.

" And the Saviour speaks in mildness ;
   ' Blest be thou of all the good !
Bear, as token of this moment,
   Marks of blood and holy rood ! '

" And that bird is called the Crossbill ;
   Covered quite with blood so clear,
In the groves of pine it singeth
   Songs, like legends, strange to hear."

THE WHITE-WINGED CROSSBILL.

CHAP. II.

The Southern Coast. — Newlyn. — Mount's Bay Boats. — Pilchard
Fishery. — Mousehole. — Landing of the Spaniards. — Merlin's
Prophecy. — Ancient Mansion of the Keigwins. — Old Dolly Pen-
treath. — Mackerel Fishery.'—Mousehole Cave. — Asplenium ma-
rinum. — St. Paul's Church. —The Glossy Ibis. — Lamorna Cove.
—Trewoofe. — Purple Heron. — Golden Oriole. — Athelstan's vic-
tory over the Cornish. — Bolleit. — The Pipers. — Cairn Bargis. —
Cairn Boscawen. — St. Loy's Cove and Chapel. — Penberth Cove.

INSTEAD of proceeding on the highway which leaves
Penzance from the west for the Logan Rock, the
tourist not unfrequently follows the line of the
southern coast by Newlyn and Mousehole. Ours is
a pedestrian tour; horses and carriages do very well
for those who are pressed for time, or for those who
merely visit a place for the sake of saying they have
been there. A hasty drive through a country scarcely
gives one a general idea of it; that which is most
worthy of observation being often in some out-of-
the-way spot, beyond the track of those who care
only to see "the lions." The reader must, therefore,
prepare himself, if he goes with us, for rough roads
and craggy paths; there will be rocks and hills to
climb, brakes of furze and fern to be pushed through,
brooks and streams, and now and then a bog, to be
crossed. So shall we meet with the most delightful

objects of nature, and gather health and strength as
we go; turning aside occasionally to examine some
legendary or storied monument; to gather some
choice plant, to observe some peculiar geological
formation, or to open the sketch-book that we may
carry away though it be but a faint memory of some
grand and impressive scene.

Passing through Street-an-Nowan we enter Newlyn,
an extensive fishing village on the shore of Gwavas
Lake; well sheltered on the west and north, but
open to the east and south-east winds. Here, at
their moorings, is a large number of the Mount's
Bay boats, among the safest and finest boats for
coast fisheries to be found anywhere. They ride
out gales which prove fatal to larger vessels. If
overtaken by a storm when on the fishing-ground, a
raft is constructed of all the loose spars and timbers
on board, this is put out at the bow so as to lie flat
on the surface of the water, thus preventing the
waves from breaking over and filling the boat. One
in a position of this kind was lost off the Land's
End in the year 1859; the first for some nineteen or twenty years past. This speaks well for
their seafaring capabilities, when we consider to
what dangers they are exposed, especially during
winter. Not long since, a crew of five men under-
took a voyage to Australia in one of them, which
they safely and rapidly performed, taking the mail
from the Cape of Good Hope. During the fishing
season the boats are run ashore occasionally for the
purpose of drying the nets; they come in at high

tide, which, as it recedes, leaves them on dry land;
in this manner they sometimes occupy the whole
line of beach from Newlyn to the Battery Rocks at
Penzance, about a mile distant.   Gulls hover around
to pick up scraps of broken fish, and sketchers are
often to be seen transferring to their canvass portions
of the busy scene; indeed, nothing can be more

MOUNT'S BAY FISHING BOATS.

picturesque than the black hulls of the boats drawn
up in a long line, with their brown sails drooping
from the masts.

A very exciting and amusing scene it is when fish
are landed at Newlyn. On the wet sand are the
noisy *Jowsters*, or hawkers, with their carts, if vehi-
cles consisting only of a pair of shafts and wheels, to
which a few baskets are lashed, can be called carts;
the fishwomen with their cowels on their backs bear-

ing away enormous loads; whilst the fishermen in their great sea-boots and oil-skins are busily occupied about the boats, nets, and sparkling fish, each eagerly pursuing his own particular work amidst a very great uproar of noisy voices. Bonnington has given some such scenes in a pleasing manner; those who like these pictures may study here from life.

Standing on the high ground over Newlyn, whence there is a glorious view of the whole bay, it is a most interesting sight, on a summer's evening, to look down on a fleet of sixty or seventy of these boats, with their rich brown sails, creeping away one after the other, out for the night's fishing. If pilchards are to be caught, the drift nets, one end being fastened to the boat, are thrown overboard in the dusk of evening and left to float with the tide: no sails are set, except during very calm weather, to prevent the nets being folded together. The fish are not enclosed in a circle but are caught in the meshes, which, being large enough to admit their heads, detain them by the gills when attempting to draw themselves back. By this mode of fishing from five to ten thousand is considered a moderate catch for one night; as many as twenty thousand are sometimes taken.

In 1851 there was a most extraordinary catch at St. Ives — one net alone was supposed to contain 16,500,000 — or 5,500 hogsheads, weighing 1100 tons. The probable value was 11,000*l*., reckoning them at the usual price of 2*l*. per hogshead before deducting expense of curing.

The seasons, of course, vary considerably. Though

a larger number than usual was not taken last year, 1860, yet it was the most profitable season the fishermen have known : the boats of Newlyn and Mousehole realised on an average not less than 200*l.* each —which to 100 boats would give a total of 20,000*l.* This success was chiefly owing to the advantages derived by direct communication by railway with London.

The fishery business is managed somewhat in the following manner : — One man builds a boat at his own cost, and perhaps provides a portion of the net —the crew also contribute so many pieces of net each, at least, all that can afford to do so, some give their labour only. The proceeds of the catch are divided according to the value of the share each one has in the affair—so that crews are not hired and paid for their labour, but every one depends on the drawing of the nets.

A net for one of the largest boats consists of fifty pieces, and stretches to the length of a mile and a half.

The regular fishery for pilchards begins towards the latter end of summer*, and is continued till late in autumn on the southern coast. These fish are very rarely seen during the winter and early spring; they are then in deep water on the south-western parts of Cornwall and the entrance to the English Channel, and to the south and west of the Scilly Islands. At this time they swim deep, rising in accordance with the calmness

* " When the corn is in the shock,
  The fish are on the rock."—*Old Cornish Rhyme.*

of the weather. Their course is generally in a westerly
direction; if the weather continues fine for some days
they are occasionally found to approach the shore in
sandy situations, as at Mount's Bay, Lamorna Cove,
and Whitsand Bay; but they rarely at this time
congregate in large masses, and frequently a few
stragglers only are to be seen. Late in the spring
and during the early part of summer they are sometimes found in small shoals, but without any definite
course. When the other fisheries have failed, advantage is taken of this their early appearance, and the
boats go in pursuit of them. But even when they
are not seen, if the nets are "shot" off the sandy
inlets about sunset, many will be frequently taken;
and what seems strange is, that they are then all
meshed on the shore side; but if taken in the
morning, on the outside of the net. From this it
appears that they approach the shore during the day
and return to deeper water towards evening. These
diurnal migrations occur when the fish are supposed
not to have arrived on our shores. As summer ad-
vances, the stragglers associate into small companies;
these again unite into larger ones called "shirmers"
or "breaking-schulls," and finally into those large
autumnal shoals which are the objects of the fishery.
In the early spring they can hardly be said to be
gregarious, for they move independently of each
other in a very irregular manner. When they begin
to congregate they rise to the surface, and though
they move about without any apparent order, yet
their general course is in a westerly direction; this is

ascertained by the side of the nets on which they are taken, and by the boats following the direction of their course. The great bulk of the fish, however, do not remain close to the shores throughout the year, but retire into deep water, and in their annual migrations they resort to the south-west, west, and north-west of Scilly, and the entrances to the Channel.

These remarks on the movements of the pilchard around the coast are gathered from a very interesting and valuable paper on the subject by Mr. R. Q. Couch.*

When landed the fish are carried to the cellars where they are salted, very regularly piled up, and submitted to heavy pressure for some weeks; they are afterwards packed into barrels for exportation, large quantities being sent to Genoa, Leghorn, Civita Vecchia, to Naples and up the Adriatic in time for the Lent fast.

The lanes around Tolcarn and the valley of Trereife, pronounced Treeve, afford very pleasant summer rambles. *Asplenium lanceolatum,* a rare and graceful fern, grows very fine at the base of Tolcarn—on the rocks, two interesting mosses are found, *Trichostomun funale* and *Pterogonium gracile.* Between Newlyn and Penlee Point, above high-water mark, are *Entosthodon Templetoni* and *Bryum Tozeri,* the latter moss, especially, is extremely rare elsewhere. In the hedge by the roadside is *Scrophularia Scoro-*

* Reports of Penzance Nat. Hist. and Antiquarian Society, vol. i.

donia ; on the hills above *Agrostis setacea,* a grass which though rare in most places is very abundant in Cornwall. Near Mousehole the following algæ have been collected; *Ectocarpus sphœrophorus, Callithamnion Brodiæi, Crouania attenuata,* and *Gloiosiphonia capillaris.*

It is impossible for a stranger in this neighbourhood to walk along the dark cliffs which fringe this side of the bay without being charmed with the loveliness of the scene. The roadway is on the very edge of the cliff, and fenced off in dangerous places by rude railings.

A short distance from Newlyn are the remains of a battery and a furnace for heating shot: these were in a more efficient state during the last French war. Penlee Point, with a pole on its summit, we notice in passing—it is a fine example of a well characterized and beautiful hornblende rock. On the line of shore from Newlyn to Mousehole, several varieties of rock are traced. They consist chiefly of hornblende and felspar in different proportions, sometimes of massive, sometimes of slaty structure. Owing to its inflections the shore is in some places parallel and in others transverse to the strata, many of which thus well displayed, come successively into view. Axinite and actinolite are often mixed with the hornblende and felspar, especially at the Lariggan Rocks, and the whole formation is striped with veins of granite, some of which are metalliferous. The productive as well as the barren varieties of these are well shown between Newlyn Pier and the point.

The derivation of the word Mousehole is uncertain. There is a large cavern in the side of the cliff known as "the Mousehole," from which some suppose the village acquired its present name. It has been considered as a corruption of the Cornish words *Môz-hayle*, the "maid's-river;" but as there is no river there this interpretation will certainly not be accepted;—another suggestion is that it is from *Moz-hal*—the "sheep's moor" and the locality is still thought to afford superior grazing for sheep. It was at one time the principal town on the shores of Mount's Bay, its ancient name being Port Enys, the "island port." The island is about a quarter of a mile from the pier; a chapel once stood on it, dedicated to St. Clement, hence its name, St. Clement's Isle. It consists of a single bed of slaty felspar, of a beautiful purple colour, containing little mica, and shows more decidedly the characters of stratification, than any single bed of the same rock on this coast.

Mousehole is famous in history as having been attacked by the Spaniards, during the reign of Queen Elizabeth. They came in four galleys and landed about two hundred men, who appear to have done considerable damage to the village, as well as to Newlyn and Penzance. As soon as Sir Francis Godolphin had induced a small company he had collected to present an aspect of resistance the enemy made off. Tradition says the Spaniards, like the French at Fishguard in Wales, were afraid to land for some time, mistaking the red cloaks of the fisherwomen for the uniforms of soldiers. The inhabitants are said to have been panic-struck more through faith in an old prophecy than for fear of the Spaniards. The fearful prediction was uttered by Merlin: thus it is in Cornish —

"Aga syth tyer, war an meyne Merlyn,
   Ara neb syth Leskey Paul, Penzance, hag Newlyn."

"There shall land on the stone of Merlin,
   Those who shall burn Paul, Penzance, and Newlyn."

Near the pier is a rock called "Merlyn Car," or "Merlin's Rock," and a little farther west is another, named the "Spaniard."

In the old mansion house, of which an illustration

THE KEIGWIN ARMS.

is given, as a good example of domestic architecture in the 16th century, is preserved a cannon ball, which is said to have killed Jenkyn Keigwin—at that time

the head of the family of that name, who appears to
have been a person of consequence in these parts.
There has also been preserved in this house an old
court dress—a coat of a light colour richly em-
broidered with red braiding.   The ceiling of one of
the rooms was ornamented with shields bearing men's
heads, dolphins, escallop shells, and other devices.
A part of the building is now used as an inn, with
the name of the " Keigwin Arms."   A member of
this family is renowned for his loyalty to the King
during the great rebellion.   One of Cromwell's
officers writes of him in a letter, as " a notable active
knave against the Parliament."   In later times there
was a Mr. John Keigwin, who possessed considerable
knowledge of the old Cornish dialect.   He wrote
some important manuscripts on the subject, which
were deposited in the Bodleian Library—and subsequently published by Davies Gilbert.   The most
celebrated character in connection with this language
is Old Dolly Pentreath, also of this place; she is
reputed to have been the last who could converse
in Cornish.   She died at the age of 102, and was
buried in Paul churchyard, where many have in vain
searched for the tombstone said to have been erected
over her remains.   The story of her epitaph is this.
A gentleman of Truro, who had studied the old
Cornish language, wrote for his amusement the following lines, which he circulated amongst his friends,
but they were never engraved on stone over Dolly's
last resting-place : —

> " Coth Doll Pentreath cans ha deau ;
>   Marow ha kledyz ed Paul plêu : —
>   Na ed an Eglos, gan pobel brâs,
>   Bes ed Eglos-hay, coth Dolly es."

In English —

> " Old Dolly Pentreath, one hundred aged and two,
>   Deceased and buried in Paul parish too :
>   Not in the church, with people great and high,
>   But in the churchyard doth old Dolly lie."

The author of this epitaph was a **Mr. Thompson,** of whom Polwhele says —" I believe he knows more of the Cornish language than the old lady whom he has celebrated ever knew, notwithstanding all that Daines Barrington has said of her."

It would certainly be a strange circumstance for the language of a country suddenly to die out with one person.   The fact is that Dolly Pentreath owes her celebrity to Daines Barrington, who, coming into Cornwall, happened to meet with this old woman.   It is most likely that she knew nothing more of the Cornish than many of her neighbours.

It is well known that Prince Lucien Bonaparte has lately been studying the dialects of England, and whilst engaged in these researches, he visited this spot to learn what remained of the Cornish.   One result of the Prince's interest in this matter may be seen at St. Paul's in the form of an inscribed granite obelisk inserted into the churchyard wall.   On the upper part is a Maltese cross, the inscription is as follows,—

" Here lieth interred Dorothy Pentreath, who died in 1778, said to have been the last person who conversed in the ancient Cornish, the peculiar language of this country from the earliest records till it expired in the eighteenth century, in this parish of St. Paul. This stone is erected by the Prince Louis Lucien Bonaparte in union with the Rev. John Garrett, vicar of St. Paul."

June, 1860.

" Honour thy father and thy mother : that thy days may be long in the land which the Lord thy God giveth thee." — (Exod. xx. 12.)

" Gwra perthi de taz ha de mam : mal de Dythiow bethewz hyr war an tyr neb an arleth de dew ryes dees." — (Exod. xx. 12.)

There can be no objection taken to the good motive of the Prince in erecting this monument. Dorothy had become celebrated, and is generally regarded as a sort of representative of the language, and doubtless many Cornishmen feel pleased with the sympathy of Prince Bonaparte on this subject.

Many Cornish words are still used by the inhabitants of the district, as well as in other parts of the county, but generally in a corrupt form. The old Celtic of Cornwall as a language may be said to have almost entirely disappeared; the names of places, however, will always retain their original appellations, and in this manner many words of the language will be preserved. In the entries of the Domesday Book and other ancient MSS. they are frequently mutilated and misspelt.

Mousehole is smaller than Newlyn, but has an excellent pier for the protection of the numerous fishing boats, which are fully employed in the pilchard and mackerel fisheries. Next to the pilchard the mackerel is the most important fish to the Cornish fishermen. They are caught nearly in the same manner as the pilchard. During autumn the fishery is carried on at a considerable distance from land, and as the mackerel is a fish which soon suffers from the heat of the weather, it is found necessary to send the catches daily to market. But, fishing so far from land, the time occupied in going to and from the markets would take more than three times as much as that employed in fishing, a waste which would be ruinous to all; for the success of a season frequently depends on three or four nights' catches, when the boats might be off their stations. To avoid this, the boats associate in companies of from five to nine, one of which takes the fish of all the others daily to market, and returns as early as possible. Each takes the office in rotation, and receives an equal share of all the fish taken during its absence. By this arrangement the fishery is never interrupted, and the greatest possible amount of success is secured. The fishery is very uncertain, for as the mackerel does not associate in such vast shoals as the pilchard, and as it is more irregular in its movements, some boats may be very successful, whilst others scarcely catch enough to pay their expenses.

Near the Mousehole, about a quarter of a mile from the village, is another platform on which cannon were mounted. It is a very difficult scramble down the face of the cliff to get at the cavern; at the entrance it is about fifty feet high; the roof is a mass of dark green, being entirely covered with ferns, which hang down in the most graceful manner; perhaps the *Asplenium marinum* grows nowhere so

fine as it does here: one specimen I gathered a short
time since measured two feet in length, but it is
frequently seen much longer; in other parts of the
kingdom where it is found its length rarely exceeds

ASPLENIUM MARINUM.

six or seven inches.   It is not confined to this particular spot, but is met with generally along the
coast, especially in caverns.

The beach here is covered with great loose rocks, very fatiguing to walk over, some of them immediately at the base of the cliff being overspread with trailing weeds which creep down from the top of the precipice, hanging about in wild luxuriance. They do not at all seem timid to approach the great waves, yet in winter they must lose the ground they gain in summer and be ruthlessly swept away. I have seen growing here, in great vigour, within a few yards of the surf, a not very common variety of the great bindweed, *Calystegia sepium,* having flowers beautifully striped with pink. *Hookeria lœtevirens* is also found in one or two caves along this part of the coast, indeed, it is the only known English habitat for this rare moss, as it is also for an Irish alga, *Cladophora Brownii.* It is a singular fact that Mr. Ralfs has met with several plants in the westernmost part of Cornwall, which are found in Ireland, but observed nowhere else in this island.

In a smaller cave at a short distance from the Mousehole, the collector of Diatoms may always meet with *Denticula tenuis.* In a cavern still farther west, *Protonema cryptarum* occurs, and on the rocks above *Pottia crinita* and *Psora atrorufa.*

At the back of Mousehole pier the junction of the slate and granite, and several interesting veins of granite in the slate, may be distinctly seen at low water.

The church of St. Paul stands on the brow of a hill just over the village, and is a very conspicuous object from the sea. The following inscription was at one

time to be seen in this church, but it has disappeared : —

"The Spanyer burnt this Church in the year 1595."

The parish register informs us that "the church,
tower, bells, and all other things pertaining to the
same, together with the houses and goods, was
burned and spoiled by the Spaniards." The porch
and an arch in the north aisle, are the only portions
left of the old church. The tower was probably
rebuilt with the materials of the original one.

There is a tablet here to the memory of one of
the Godolphin family, some ancient pieces of armour
are preserved near it. Cornish inscriptions are said
to have been numerous at one time on the walls of
the churches in the western part of the county ; if
so, they have been removed, and I am not aware
that any exist in the churches in this district, except
at St. Paul, where the following lines are on a monument, inscribed to Captain Stephen Hutchins.

"Bownas heb dueth Eu poes karens wei,
Tha Pobl Bohadzak Paull han Egles nei."

All writers agree that this church was not dedicated
to the great Apostle; some say it was named in
honour of St. Paul de Leon, a native of Cornwall,
who founded many monasteries, and was very successful in converting the pagans of Brittany; others
rightly claim the honour for St. Paulinus, first Arch-
bishop of York, who was sent by Pope Gregory into
England, soon after the mission of St. Augustin. In
the "Valor Ecclesiasticus," temp. Henry VIII., the

name of the church is spelt Poule, and in the taxation of Pope Nicholas A.D. 1291, it is entered as
" Ecclesia Sancti Paulini."   The last authority is decisive of the question of the dedication.   The church
belonged to the Abbey of Hayles in Gloucester.

Kerris Roundago, an elliptical structure of Celtic
days, is more than a mile west of the church.   It is
not much out of the way from the high road to
Lamorna; indeed, this track will be found of much
interest, particularly so to the botanist.   Kerris
Moor, which must be passed, affords many species of
Diatomaceæ and Desmidieæ.   On Trevelloe Cairn,
itself worthy of a visit, are rare lichens; *Sticta
scrobiculata, Cetraria sepincola, Alectoria jubata,*
and *Parmelia diatrypa.*   On Castallack Cairn, which

THE GLOSSY IBIS.

is nearer Lamorna, may be found *Andræa Rothii*
and *Jungermannia setacea.*

The mountain linnet and glossy ibis have been captured in the parish of St. Paul, the latter, a bird seldom seen in this country, is also known to have visited the Isles of Scilly.

Starting from Mousehole and following the edge of the cliffs, we shall have difficult and boggy ground to pass between the Mousehole cave and Penzer point. A little to the east of Cairn Kimyel is a

LAMORNA COVE.

large cavern, called "Giant's Cave," it is about forty feet high, and runs in to a depth of a hundred feet; at the mouth, the roof is formed of angular granite stones and clay; in the middle it is of solid granite. Cairn du, the "Black Cairn," forms the eastern extremity of Lamorna Cove.

Long before we reach Lamorna, we hear the ringing of the workmen's tools, and the explosions by which the granite is riven for use. The *jumper*, the tool employed for boring the rock, is simply a long bar of iron pointed with steel; large quantities of gunpowder are used, and one slice of granite thus split off is sometimes large enough to form the side of a moderate sized house. Of course such ponderous masses cannot be removed, and they must be again blasted into smaller pieces. A block taken from the quarries in 1851, was wrought to an obelisk and sent to the Great Exhibition, its height was upwards of 22 feet, its weight 21 tons. Several men are employed in working the blocks into regular forms, ready for depositing in their respective positions in buildings, and large quantities are used in public works throughout the kingdom. A stage was erected and vessels were laden at the cove, but as it is rather a dangerous place for navigation,—the vessels being only able to get in with certain winds, — the practice appears lately to have been abandoned, and the stone is drawn on waggons to Penzance, whence it is shipped. The granite quarries of Lamorna are among the most important in Cornwall; the granite is of very superior quality, but it is remarkable that that on the eastern side of the valley is alone valuable; the frequent occurrence of quartz veins on the western side renders the granite unfit for building purposes where large masses are required; some veins of this coarser kind extend across the valley. The porphyritic granite, which is studded with large crystals of felspar, sometimes two or three inches in length, producing a very singular appearance, will be seen here in great abun-

dance, whilst the natural joints of the rock cannot
fail to strike the most casual observer; these ma-
terially facilitate the progress of the workman.

Many rare lichens enrich the rocks at Lamorna,
such as *Parmelia diatrypa* and *speciosa*, *Roccella
tinctoria*, *Lecidea stellulata* and *Lecanora aipospila*.
The *Roccella fuciformis* was formerly abundant and
fine, on some rocks on the eastern side, but has been
destroyed in prosecuting the quarry works; it may
still be found along the coast between the cove and
the Logan Rock.

The valley of Lamorna runs up a considerable
distance into the country; it is a very picturesque
spot, especially this lower part, where trees form
shady arches over the little stream which here divides the parishes of St. Paul and St. Buryan; nearer
the shore fine piles of granite wreathed in garlands
of ivy rear their heads

" High o'er the river's darksome bed."

The stream twists and turns around great rocks, and
the little waterfalls in its course are as well worthy
the attention of the artist as those seen on large
rivers.   A short way up, amid the dense foliage, we
catch a glimpse of the water flashing over a mill-
wheel; we then follow along a " green lane," which
is little traversed.   Trewoofe, or, as it is commonly
called Trove, is situate in this woody land; it lies
near the high road which leads from Paul to the
southern parts of St. Buryan, and which would have
been the nearest route to the Logan Rock if we had
not intended to visit Lamorna and the coast.

The doorway of the ancient mansion house of Trewoofe is curious, the jambs being quaintly carved
with figures and devices, and the arms of the Trevalis
family are over the arch.

On this estate are the remains of a triple in-
trenchment, a subterranean passage is connected
with it, in which, it is said, during the rebellion a

THE PURPLE HERON.

party of Royalists hid themselves from the troopers
of Fairfax.

This charming valley resounds in the summer time
with the songs of birds, and it is a spot well known
to the sportsman, as the first flights of woodcocks are
often marked by their being seen on their arrival in
this valley, which about a quarter of a mile farther

on expands itself into a broad bottom, varied with
cultivated and swampy ground, and frequented in
winter by snipes, wading-birds, and wild-fowl of
various species : including wild duck, widgeon, teal,
pintail ducks, shovellers, pochards, tufted ducks,
golden eyes, &c. ; according to the intensity and
duration of the frost. Amongst the waders, the
common heron, bitterns occasionally, and one of the
rarest and most beautiful of the tribe, the purple

THE GOLDEN ORIOLE.

heron, have been obtained from this spot. Besides
the common snipe, several species of the sandpiper
are found in this locality, including the common
sandpiper, as well as the redshank, and dusky sandpipers. At Trevelloe, close by Trewoofe, a beautiful
British bird, the golden oriole, was captured during
the past summer, and of which, on account of its
rarity, it has been thought proper to give an illustration. The body is of a very deep yellow, almost

approaching orange; the greater portions of the wings and tail are black.

We follow the road westward, perhaps, in the very footsteps of Athelstan and his soldiers, who, centuries ago, advanced to meet the Cornish at Bolleit, where it is said, the last struggle was made. The Britons had for some time been driven beyond the Tamar, but in this western extremity they had maintained their own. And now came the Saxon king to add the westernmost parts of the land to his dominion.

The result is well known, the battle was decisive, the Saxon victorious; and two great pillars of granite, the one fifteen and a half, the other thirteen and a half feet high, and about three hundred yards asunder, which are still to be seen here, are said to have been erected by Athelstan to mark the scene of conflict, and to commemorate the story of his triumph. Henceforth, the place was called Bolleit, "the place of slaughter."

Here, it is conjectured, was the ancient court-house of the hundred, this being a royal estate extending to the Land's End.

Long after this battle, the Cornish had their own kings and dukes. They appear to have been permitted to hold this position, rather than to have maintained it by their own power, for the very act of Althestan in founding a large religious establishment at Buryan and granting privileges in connection with it, which were long retained, shows that he must have had authority over this part of the country.

At Bolleit, or rather on Rosemoddress estate adjoining, is a Druidic circle, originally consisting of nineteen stones, some of which are fallen. It is popularly called the "Dawns Myin," the "dancing stones," the tradition being that these were young women turned into stone for dancing on the Lord's

THE PIPERS.

day. And the two granite pillars, in a field across the road, which we have already noticed, were the "Pipers" petrified for a like offence. Dr. Borlase imagined that these pillars served some purpose of the Druids in connection with the circle. If they were not erected by Athelstan, they are most probably sepulchral monuments. Barrows have been opened near this place and urns and ashes found within them. At Bolleit, too, is an old British cave, in which it is supposed the natives secreted their goods or hid themselves in times of danger.

It has been attempted to make Bolleit into Bollait, and to interpret it as a French or Norman word signifying the "dairy" or "milk-cot," but it is not likely that such an important place would bear a name with such an insignificant meaning. A Norman family, which might have taken name from this estate, resided here, and there is a curious monument to one of the family in St. Buryan Church.

Near Bolleit is a "holed stone," thought to have served some purpose of the Druids, now used as a gate-post; near it is an ancient wayside cross.

About three quarters of a mile south of Bolleit is Boscawen-rose, which place gave name to the noble Cornish family of Boscawen, of which was the celebrated admiral, "the glory not only of Cornwall, but of his country." Boscawen-rose, in Cornish, is said to mean, "the house of the elder-tree* valley," but another interpretation gives it as *Bos*, a house, *Saissan*, Saxon, and that a Saxon fort was constructed here, on the reduction of West Cornwall by Athelstan, and maintained as a bridle and curb on the natives. It is not my intention to trouble the reader unnecessarily with the meanings of Cornish words, but it will be seen that they are important, as they are either expressive of characteristics of locality or confirmative of history.

We quitted the wild sea-shore at Lamorna to introduce the reader to the interesting monuments

* Elder-tree, anciently called a skew-tree; hence *skewer*.

at Bolleit, whence a tolerably direct road leads to Penberth Cove and the Logan Rock; but we shall resume our walk by the cliffs.

The next prominent object after leaving Lamorna Cove is a conical hill called Cairn Bargis, the "kite's cairn;" kites build about here, and buzzards and hawks are numerous around the coast, where they find secure nooks for their nests in the lofty and rugged peaks, inaccessible save to birds. Rosemoddress Cairn is back from the coast. A patch of slate here over-lies the granite, but as it is very small and offers no peculiarities it needs no detailed description. Two rocks just off the shore are called the Bucks. A fine headland now rises before us named the Black-rock; here garnets have been found. At Cairn Silver, the granite recommences. We shall notice also veins of schorl rock, which is supposed by some geologists to be rather a variety of granite than a distinct rock; although difficult of working, it has been wrought into form and when polished has a beautiful appearance. At Cairn Boscawen about a mile and a half farther on is a very large vein of this rock, forming a pro-minent object in the almost perpendicular cliff; it is visible from high water mark to the height of about sixty feet.

The rocks at Cairn Boscawen are piled up in a very extraordinary manner; at one place is a curious opening; beneath this "pensile stone" Dr. Borlase conjectured the Arch-Druid might have sat and delivered his decisions and predictions. No one can say it was not used for such a purpose, the Druids adopted imposing masses of rock to produce a greater effect, and they may as well have used this as any other. Then again it is pleasant to rest here in the sunshine on the beautiful green sward, above the blue sea, and look into the ages back, and fancy these awful priests gliding in a mysterious manner about the Cairn, performing some peculiar ceremony; and we cannot but feel obliged to the Doctor for his speculations, which have cast a halo of romance around the spot; combining with the grandeur of the scene, it leaves a lasting impression on the mind. The crags and bold outline of Castle Treryn are seen to advantage from here.

On account of rough and boggy ground the tourist will be prevented from skirting the cliff from Boscawen to St. Loy's Cove. It will, therefore, be necessary to go inland a little, nearly up to Boskenna "the house upon an ascent;" we shall then come down through the wooded valley, by the side of "a little nameless stream." This will amply repay for the lengthened walk, for it is truly a romantic valley, and affords a striking contrast to other portions of the coast we shall go over, especially to the cold and dreary north. The trees extend to the verge of the cliff, a strange combination of luxuriant foliage with wild and savage rocks against which the waves are ever beating. Embowered amidst the trees is a cottage, before the door a little garden,—

> "most for use design'd,
> Yet not of beauty destitute."

A beautiful little plant, *Wahlenbergia hederacea,*

grows in moist places, and by the side of streams such as that which wends down this valley. Its

WAHLENBERGIA HEDERACEA.

flowers are of a pale blue; when grown in greenhouses it soon overspreads, and hangs gracefully around the sides of the flower-pot; cultivated in this manner it flowers abundantly, and for simplicity and elegance may vie with the more gaudy and costly exotics.

The reason the cove is called St. Loy's is this:—Centuries ago, when men's ways were more simple than now, when their wants were less,—when their piety and devotion were great,—it was the custom with some of the good and devout, to erect a chapelry,

which served them as a hermitage, and there they
dwelt alone, in solitary and secluded spots; yet was
the odour of their sanctity diffused around, and the
penitent performed pilgrimages, and the people came,
to receive consolation and instruction where the
Christian altar had been raised. Such chapels were
numerous in Cornwall, especially by the coast in the
western part; and of the Fathers who occupied
them, thus has it been well sung by one of Cornwall's
poets:—

> " They had their lodges in the wilderness,
>   Or built them cells beside the shadowy sea,
>   And there they dwelt with angels, like a dream !
>   So they unclosed the volume of the Book,
>   And filled the fields of the Evangelist,
>   With thoughts, as sweet as flowers ! "

A chapel of this kind, stood on the verge of the
cliff in this cove; it was dedicated to St. Eloy*, of
whom Chaucer speaks in his Canterbury Tales. A
few years since the remains of this little building,
with its stone altar, were to be seen; they have since
been toppled into the sea, that a few feet of land
might be gained for early crops. How forcibly does
this act of destruction contrast with the meekness
and piety which raised the structure, with the " days
of eld " and our present utilitarian age, in which
perhaps too many temples are sacrificed to gain.

It should be stated that the ruins of St. Eloy's
chapel were swept away without permission from the
proprietor of the land.

* The French breviate for S. Eligius, Bishop of Noyon, A.D. 659.

The geologist will perceive a raised beach here.
Merthen Point extends from the western extremity
of the cove. "Merthen," is Cornish for "pool." The
next indentation in the coast is Porguarnon, which
is enclosed by hills, giving the place somewhat the
appearance of an amphitheatre; hence its name. We
then come on Pednsawanack, so called probably
from the cavern there; this headland forms the
eastern side of Penberth Cove, where there are a few

PENBERTH COVE.

fishermen's cottages; the boats, except when in use,
are drawn up the landing place, which is paved with
large stones, and fastened to iron rings in the rocks.

Old pieces of wreck, crab-pots, oars, masts, nets, and miscellaneous *débris*, such as sketchers like to meet with, are plentifully scattered around. On my last visit to this spot, there was an old boat with one side resting on the declivity of the hill, the other side supported by rude posts, thus forming a shed, the objects under it being in keeping—presenting altogether a characteristic sea-side study.

Penberth valley is in some respects similar to those of Lamorna and St. Loy. There is a very pretty little glen a short distance from the shore, in which two or three cottages are hidden; their existence is betrayed to the eye of the tourist perhaps by the curling of the smoke through the trees. Just over the eastern side of the cove is a curious group of rock, which, from some positions, looks like a tower with four pinnacles, thus it has acquired the name of " the church."

The stream here divides the parishes of St. Buryan and St. Levan. The point on the west side of the cove shown in the woodcut, is called Cribba Head, "the Crested Head; " it will be seen that the rocks on the summit resemble, somewhat, the crest or comb of a bird. On mounting this hill we find that we are approaching wilder and more magnificent scenes; we almost *feel* the presence of the stupendous crags and peaks of Castle Treryn, which is now distinctly seen, towering above all the other headlands. Before we reach it, several objects are passed worthy of notice. First Cairn Keg, with " cheese-like rocks." Cairn Clog, the " Cairn of hard rock," and Point

Whiscan is very fine; then comes a creek called Haldinas Cove, which means "the cove near the Castled Hill." A rent in the cliff is called Zawn Groynia. Groyne is a seal; this animal probably having been seen here. On the eastern side of the promontory of Treryn is the Gamper and the Seghs Rock,—Segh, probably a corruption of Shagga: thus it would be the Shag's or Cormorant's rock.

This brings us to the narrow pass at Castle Treryn, the site of the famous Logan Rock.

THE ROSE-COLOURED PASTOR.

CHAP. III.

As there are so many objects of interest to be seen and described in the interior, it will be necessary to leave the coast for a time.

The Land's End, following the carriage road from Penzance, is about ten miles distant. Hundreds of visitors pass over this road in the summer time, and we also will now take this route, not hesitating to step aside occasionally to inspect some curious monument or legendary spot.

The beautifully wooded grounds of Trereife, about a mile from the town, first attract attention ; the roadway is here arched with a long avenue of noble elms ; near its extremity it is crossed by another avenue, — the road turning from the left leads to Newlyn, — a

few yards up on the right is Trereife House, almost
buried in foliage; a yew tree is trained over the front
of the building, giving it the appearance of a living
wall of leaves. The rooks have long been established
here in their " old ancestral trees," and we always
know when spring is coming by their noisy prepara-
tions for building. The walks and peeps of woodland
scenery around this place are very beautiful. The
Sibthorpia Europœa, previously noticed, is met with
here again, as it is indeed in almost every rill in the
district.

On the ascent of a hill, a little beyond Trereife, an
old oak forms a complete archway over the road, and
if you are on the seat of the carriage beside the
driver, he will probably tell you that it is the only
instance of the kind to be met with on the journey
from London to the Land's End. A short distance
from this, on the left hand side of the road, stands an
ancient cross; such monuments are very numerous
throughout the county, but more particularly in this
western part. They are pleasing and picturesque
objects by the wayside, reminding us of interesting
periods of our history. The crosses in this district
are probably the most ancient of any in England.
Some of the earliest examples were perhaps set up
by Christians on those spots which were previously
sacred to Druidic ceremonies. It has been asserted
that the Gospel was introduced into Cornwall even
during apostolic times, consequently, long before the
visit of St. Patrick from Ireland; and it is evident
that there was a British church established in Cornwall and Wales, which long maintained its indepen-

dence of Rome. It is well known these Christians
strongly opposed the bishops appointed to this

WAYSIDE CROSS.

country by Rome. Aldhelm, the first bishop of the
western part of England, is said to have sent severe
reprimands to Geruntius, king of the Cornish, because
the British monks would not observe some peculiar
ceremonies according to the ritual of the Roman
Church.

At a very remote period Cornwall had frequent
and direct communication with Eastern countries
whence the Christian religion was diffused, and this
probably accounts for their early acquaintance with
the faith. The greater number of these crosses have
the Greek form, showing that those who erected them
had some connection with the Eastern Church. But
it is probable that many of these monuments are of

British origin, and may date back to the third or
fourth century, or even earlier. The most ancient
crosses are mere rude stone shafts with circular heads,
on which is carved a cross shaped like the Greek or
Maltese; there are also many of the Latin form, some
of them, most likely, set up during the progress of the
Irish missionaries. In succeeding periods different
forms were adopted, the later examples having figures
carved on them, and being richly ornamented in the
Gothic style. They were erected for various purposes; in early ages when there were no regular
roads through the country, many were placed on
dreary moors to direct the traveller on his way; and
tradition tells of a pleasing and charitable custom of
those days—that the rich traveller often deposited
alms on these crosses for the succour of the weary
and distressed wayfarer who might follow him. They
served also as prayer stations, and to guide the pilgrim to the different baptisteries and oratories, and
many are still found by the pathways leading to the
churches.

Buryas Bridge is at the foot of the hill; it consists
of three arches, and spans as pretty a trout stream
as one needs to angle in. It is not broad enough to
throw a fly on, and a sportsman might pass it with
contempt, yet river trout of good size have been
landed on its banks. This stream wanders through
various scenes, by bleak granite hills and furze
brakes: it rises near the Mên Scryfa, is overlooked
by wild cairns and curious monuments; and if we
could understand its murmurs, it might be telling of

the old streamers who worked by its banks — of the warlike tribes and strangely attired men who have crossed its course. It is bordered sometimes by

BURYAS BRIDGE.

masses of purple heath, and sweetly scented wild flowers; it splashes over mill-wheels, too, and forms pretty waterfalls over moss-covered rocks; it is crossed by other rustic bridges, but perhaps none so picturesque as this at Buryas, which is partly clad with ivy and shaded by an ash tree. The rural appearance of the scene is enhanced by the adjacent cottages also dressed in ivy; the smoke from the chimneys appearing to rise from masses of green leaves; roses and creepers hang all about the little windows, and the flowers in the gardens grow most luxuriantly.

The stream now glides down the fertile and wooded valley of Trereife.

Here we leave the slate and enter on the granite tract which extends to the cliffs.

A few yards from the bridge is the entrance to

> " a shady avenue,
> Where lofty elms abound."

This conducts us into Nancothan, the " Old Valley ; " two mills here, one standing just over the other, are sufficiently dilapidated for the sketcher, and seem to be favourite subjects with artistic tourists.

On reaching the summit of the ascent, on the Land's End road, and looking eastward, a portion of the bay will be seen shut in by hills, giving it the appearance of a lake, with St. Michael's Mount in the midst.

At Drift are two monumental stones and an ancient cross. A road leads hence to Sancreed Church.

The country now assumes a more open and exposed aspect; trees and plantations will not be met with again in the journey westward; the hills are grey with rocks, the downs are covered with furze and heath ; there is little shelter to be found by the roadside, and a pitiless tract it is to the traveller if he be overtaken by a storm. This is a striking contrast to the beautiful valley of Nancothan just left behind, but it may be taken as characteristic of the county, which is a repetition of desert and oasis. A stranger would be struck with these sudden changes, at one moment finding himself in a most lovely and picturesque valley, fertile and richly wooded; at the next, entering on a dreary and barren common, surrounded by bleak hills and rough cairns. It is certainly more agreeable to the tourist to pass through a district so varied, than to be wearied by constantly travelling through cultivated lands;— the contrast enhances the value of each.

After leaving Drift the road twists and turns in a peculiar serpentine manner,—at one turn we may be facing the sun, at the next it may be almost behind us. We shall observe other roads similarly formed; whether they were so constructed from any superstitious motive, or from the irregular division of land, we shall not stay to inquire.

Just as the road gets out of its convolutions, there is a directing post and a wayside inn. This spot is called Catch-all, probably from the chance this house has of catching all who pass by. The road up the hill on the left leads to St. Buryan, St. Levan, and the Logan Rock, the other to the Land's End. After proceeding on the latter for about half a mile, a tall granite pillar will be observed in the corner of a field adjoining the road; it is on the Trego-nebris estate, and, like those we have seen at Bolleit, must be considered sepulchral, or as a memorial of some important but forgotten event. The road ascends a little after leaving this, and, arriving on higher ground, the tourist, by standing on the hedge on the left, will perceive between him and St. Buryan church, the celebrated Druidic circle of Boscawen-ûn. It is about half a mile distant, and

may be approached by striking across the common
or by following a rugged roadway.   Nineteen stones
originally formed the circle, but two or three have
fallen ; there is also a tall stone in the centre.   Dr.

BOSCAWEN-ÛN CIRCLE.

Borlase considered these circles to have been places
of council or judgment, and of this one he says,
" Whilst any election or decree was depending, or any
solemn compact to be confirmed, the principal
persons concerned stood each by his pillar, and where
a middle stone was erected in the circle, there stood
the prince or general elect."   It has been the custom
with some writers when alluding to Dr. Borlase's
remarks on such subjects, to treat them as idle
dreams or worthless speculations ; but we must remember that this great antiquary studied particularly

the customs of the Druids, and his observations were always founded on his acquaintance with ancient authors and with what had been recorded of that strange priesthood. Thus many of his theories startle those who are unacquainted with such matters, whilst others assume to be offended with his writings, rather than confess their own ignorance of the subjects which he has treated. Now there is an ancient Welsh triad which in some respects confirms the notion Dr. Borlase had of this very circle. In English it is as follows : — " The three Gorsedds of Poetry of the Island of Britain; the Gorsedd of Boscawen in Damnonium * ; the Gorsedd of Salisbury in England ; and the Gorsedd of Bryn Gwyddon in Wales." This translation is by an eminent Welsh scholar and antiquary, the late Rev. Thomas Price. " I do not hesitate," he says, " to translate Beiscawen (as it is in the original), Boscawen in Cornwall, between Penzance and the Land's End, near which are some Druidical remains, especially a stone circle." Gorsedd means a place of judgment. Thus this was one of the three principal places in Britain for the judgment of poetry, and must have been particularly connected with that class of Druids called " Bards," whose business it was to celebrate the praises of their heroes in songs composed and sung to their harps.

In going to or returning from the circle a pile of rock is passed on which are several cavities, two of

---

* Devon and Cornwall were once united under this name.

them resembling the impressions of human feet, but much larger; they are called the "Giant's footsteps." The cairn is known by the name of Careg or Creeg Tol—the "holed rock." In the eastern part of the county any wonderful appearance in the works of nature is generally attributed to King Arthur; thus a hollow in a rock, similar to these, but of greater dimensions, is called King Arthur's Bed, and two smaller depressions were made by his dogs lying beside him. Being overtaken by night whilst hunting, he had used a huge rock as his bed. In these western parts, which it appears Arthur did not visit much, the giants have the credit of such works, for it is the tradition of the country that a much larger race of men stalked over this ground than any that are now to be seen. They appear to have amused themselves by hurling great rocks, hundreds of tons weight, from hill to hill, and singular hollows are yet to be seen, sunk by their fingers, so firmly did they grasp the stone. By the vibrations of their laughter and shouts great fissures were shaken in the cliffs; and some of the highest crags of the cairns fell down. Large stones are sometimes found arranged in peculiar order; these were tossed about for some game: sometimes they are scattered about in confusion; there was some fierce battle fought: then, as we have seen, they left their footprints in the solid rock whilst springing from cairn to cairn. The numerous Cromlêhs were the giant's quoits, affording them agreeable pastime to topple down by pitching at them rocks which now require powerful machinery to move. The lofty granite pillars we have noticed at Bolleit and elsewhere marked the sites of their graves. Thus was the land possessed by monstrous men, of whose size we can only conjecture from these singular appearances. They do not appear to have been wicked; nothing is said of cruel deeds performed, their chief business seems to have been to throw about and overturn huge rocks, a little disagreement sometimes giving rise to a quarrel. Upon the whole they were well behaved for giants.

On regaining the high road, the dark hills of Bartiné and Cairn Brea will be seen away to the right. At Crowz-an-wra, roads branch off to St. Buryan and St. Just. A curious old cross stands here. Crowz-an-wra is Cornish for the " cross by the wayside."

A mile farther on, adjoining the road, is an old burial ground, formerly used by the Quakers; a wooden post stands by the wall; the surrounding country is open and unsheltered, the graves are entirely covered by thorns and briars ; and we know not what could have induced the selection of such a spot for such a purpose, unless those who were buried there wished to be laid beyond the reach of human sympathy. Hence to Sennen Church the road is tolerably level. Another wayside cross will be observed built into a hedge on Sennen Green. Whitsand Bay lies open on the right; the long horizontal line of the sea stretches beyond the land, and the moaning of the waves is faintly heard, as they are cast back from the invulnerable cliffs.

Sennen Church, dedicated to St. Senanus, a holy

man of Irish celebrity, is a low weather beaten
structure, and harmonises well with the wild and
romantic region in which it stands.   Being 390 feet
above the level of the sea, it forms a conspicuous

SENNEN CHURCH.

object for many miles around.   It consists of a nave
and chancel, with a side chapel, in which a rude
figure of alabaster, belonging to some ancient monument, still remains.   Externally, the character of the
building has been much marred by the insertion of
ugly modern windows, and the interior is in a most
dilapidated state, calling loudly for restoration.   The
objects most worthy of notice, are, the font and an
old " low-side-window," commonly, but erroneously,
called a Lychnoscope.   The latter is late, and of the
sixteenth century, but is remarkable for the fact,
that it is said to have been used down to a comparatively recent period for the delivery of a certain
tithe, or " due," once a year.   The Font is chiefly
curious for the inscription around its base, which is

imbedded in the pavement. At one time it stood
within the altar rails, whence it was removed to its
original and correct position. Hals gives the following account of it; after speaking of some effigies
which the sexton had pointed out to him, he goes on
to say—" He also showed me an inscription on the
foot of the font stone, which, he told me, several
bishops of Exeter and their priests in their triennial
visitations at Buryan and this church had viewed,
but could not read it: whereupon, in like manner, I
observed on the font stone the said inscription, in a
barbarous strange character of letters, of which I
could see but part, by reason of a new pew or seat
which was built on a part of it: however I interpreted
that which I saw to consist of these letters, Anno
Dom. Mille CCCCXX. or XL., in the year of our
Lord 1420 or 1440. Let the curious remove the
seat and explain the rest; probably this church was
then erected." This inscription is of the fifteenth
century, and in the letters and with the usual abbre-
viations of the period. A portion of it has been
broken away, the remainder appears to be as follows:
" Eccla ì decołe S. I. B. dedica fvit anno dni millo
CCCCOXLI," in full, " Hæc Ecclesia in decollatione
Sancti Johannis Baptistæ dedicata fuit Anno Domini
Millesimo quadringentesimo quadragesimo primo "
(secundo, tertio, or quarto, for it seems likely that
the remainder of the date has been broken away
with the missing fragment); which is in English—
" This church was dedicated on the festival of the
beheading of St. John the Baptist, A. D. 1441."

East of the church, a few yards from the roadside, and near the end of a small cottage, is the Table-mên — a block of granite seven feet ten inches long, and three feet high, which has probably given name

TABLE-MÊN.

to the estate on which it stands. Main or mên, is Cornish for " stone." This was used, according to tradition, as a dining-table by some Saxon kings, who either for business or pleasure came to this famed spot. Some say there were three kings only; others speak of seven. Hals has given their names as follows : — " Ethelbert, fifth king of Kent; Cissa, second king of the south Saxons; Kingills, sixth king of the west Saxons; Sebert, third king of the east Saxons; Ethelfred, seventh king of the North-umbers; Penda, ninth king of the Mercians; and

Sigebert, fifth king of the east Angles; who all flourished about the year 600." Merlin, who appears to have had something to say about every nook in the kingdom, has prophesied that a yet larger number of kings will assemble around this rock for a similar purpose, previously to some great event, or the destruction of the world itself. As before-mentioned, a rock near the Lanyon Cromlêh, claims this honour, and a similar story is attached to another at Bosavern in the parish of St. Just.

The inn at Sennen village is called "The First and

THE FIRST AND LAST INN IN ENGLAND.

Last Inn in England." On the western side of the sign is, "The First Inn in England," on the eastern side, "The Last Inn in England."

The Land's End is still a mile distant; the road is more pleasant to walk, than to be driven over; walking, we not only escape the jolts to which the carriage is subjected in passing over the rocks which rise above the surface; but we may botanise by the way. The *Illecebrum verticillatum*, which may almost be

ILLECEBRUM VERTICILLATUM.

called a Cornish plant, will be particularly noticed; it spreads profusely over damp ground, and with its delicately-pointed white flowers encircling the stem, manages to make itself attractive, although small.

We had seen the sea like a line of mist when some

miles back on the road; now the vessels as they pass around the promontory are distinctly visible, and the sound of the waves is louder. What a solemn sound it is, that " never-ceasing murmur of the waves, that voice which for countless ages has never been silent, but day and night for evermore, beats time with its melancholy music." The mysterious appearance and awful noises of the sea must certainly have a strong impression on those who set eyes on it for the first time — an impression which those accustomed to the seaside do not feel; and if the reader has never beheld the ocean, there is no more fitting place than the Land's End to introduce him to it. Here the waves will be seen in their most terrible grandeur, driven home by the might of the great Atlantic.

Just on the brow of the slope which runs down to the Land's End, is a house belonging to "the First and Last," where carriages and horses remain, whilst the visitors ramble about the cliffs. The ground inclines rapidly from this spot to the head of the promontory.

Some years ago an officer attempted to ride here on horseback. The story has been often told, and many different versions have been given. The following is authentic, as it was written by General Sir Robert Arbuthnot himself:—

"In June, 1804, when captain in a dragoon regiment, and aide-de-camp to General Wilford, who was stationed at Falmouth, I attended him on an inspection of a yeomanry corps at Penzance. The day after the expedition, the General, with a party, proceeded to the Land's End on an excursion of pleasure, and after taking refreshment at a house known by the name of 'The First and Last Inn in England,' three of the party, consisting of myself, Lieut. Cubitt of the Royal Artillery, and a clergyman who resided at Marazion, preceded the others, and on arriving at the top of the slope reaching down to the extremity of the Land's End, on each side of which was a steep precipice, I perceived that the grass was short and slippery, and although a dragoon officer, I did not think it prudent to ride down; but my two companions being of a different opinion did so, when I followed them leading my horse. After remaining a short time at the bottom, we mounted to regain the General, who had with his party reached the spot, whence we had started, and were astonished, especially the General, at seeing me at the bottom of the hill, and terrified at what afterwards occurred. Although I did not think it prudent to ride down, I fancied there could be no danger in riding up; and accordingly I mounted, but we had not proceeded far, when my mare, a very spirited animal, became unruly, in consequence of the girths of the saddle going back, and she began to kick and plunge, inclining to the precipice on the right. Although in imminent danger, I did not, happily, lose my presence of mind, and I threw myself off when not more than four feet from the edge of the cliff. Mine was a hussar saddle, and the bridle having a whip at the end of it, I threw it over the mare's head, and was able to keep hold of it and to check her, so as to prevent her kicking me.

When she turned with her back to the cliff, I let her
go, and she fell down and was dashed to pieces, leaving
me on the ground close to the edge of the cliff. A
person went down in a basket and brought up the
shattered saddle and bridle, which a saddler at Penzance begged me to give him that he might hang it
at the door of his shop. Many accounts of the event
were circulated, but this is the true one."

The mark of the horse's hoof on the turf was for a
long time after kept cleared out, and shown to
visitors by the guides who loiter about the place.

The accompanying view of the Land's End is
taken from near the spot where this circumstance
occurred.

The extreme point of the Land's End promontory
is about sixty feet above the sea. It exhibits one
of the finest instances of the columnar form of
granite. The rocks on the summit are piled up in
singular order — assuming prismatic and cubical
forms, at the base they resemble somewhat the
Giant's Causeway in Ireland; this appearance, however, is only to be seen during low water. The cliffs
are very precipitous, almost perpendicular, and continue so along the whole coast, especially to the
south. A large cavern, called the Land's End Hole,
in Cornish, Vau-Laz, about a hundred and fifty feet in
length, runs directly through the promontory, and
can be got at during low water, under the direction
of a guide; the sea flows through it, and it is said
that boats have passed from one side to the other;
but it seems too narrow in the middle, and had it

been wide enough, the sea must be very calm indeed
to permit such a feat — calmer than it is often seen
at this place, where the waves are seldom at rest.
Yet have I looked down on the water beneath these
rocks when it has been almost motionless, a gentle
swell would just upheave the surface occasionally,
and then subside, like the breathing of a monstrous
living thing,—

> " the restless
> Heart of the ocean
> Was for a moment consoled."

The weeds at the bottom were distinctly seen
waving gently to and fro,—

> " The yellow and scarlet tufts of ocean
> Were bending like corn on the upland lea,"

and the sea imparted a greenish hue, a most delicate
emerald, to the great white rocks that lay there ; fish
were sporting about close to the shore, their fins
rippling and rising above the surface sometimes.
This was a rare chance to see the Land's End so
tranquil. It was one of the hottest days in July, and
not a breath of wind astir. Visitors might come and
go a hundred times and not find it so. For the general
appearance of the sea is restless and broken around
these rocks, being almost always " laced with white
foam from the eternal surge." The grandest effects
of the waves are not always to be seen, as many
might suppose, during hard wind, but frequently in
calm weather, when the heavy ground seas come in in

a very imposing manner, and break thunderingly on
the rocks. Sheets of spray rise to an immense height
and fall again perpendicularly; the roaring sound is
re-echoed through the lofty caverns, and fearfully
cast back from the great walls of the cliffs. Then is
heard the hissing and boiling of the water as it rushes
back preparing for the next attack. It is truly a
sublime sight to behold the mighty billows in their
anger dashing on such a coast as this, and one cannot
watch their baffled rage without being reminded of
that Almighty One by whom they are governed, who
hath " placed the sand for the bound of the sea by a
perpetual decree, that it cannot pass it; and though
the waves thereof toss themselves, yet can they not
prevail; though they roar yet can they not pass over
it."

In his criticism on Turner's picture of the Land's
End, Mr. Ruskin says:—"At the Land's End there is
to be seen the entire disorder of the surges, when
every one of them, divided and entangled among
promontories as it rolls, and beaten back post by post
from walls of rock on this side and that side, recoils
like the defeated division of a great army, throwing
all behind it into disorder, breaking up the succeeding
waves into vertical ridges, which, in their turn, yet
more totally shattered upon the shore, retire in more
hopeless confusion, until the whole surface of the sea
becomes one dizzy whirl of rushing, writhing, tor-
tured, undirected rage, bounding, and crashing, and
coiling in an anarchy of enormous power, subdivided
into myriads of waves, of which every one is not, be

it remembered, a separate surge, but part and portion of a vast one, actuated by eternal power, and giving in every direction the mighty undulation of impetuous line, which glides over the rocks and writhes in the wind, overwhelming the one and piercing the other with the form, fury, and swiftness of a sheet of lambent fire."

Other eminent painters, as well as Turner, have visited the Land's End to study effects of sea and the breaking of waves on a rocky coast, and had they searched the world over they might not have found a spot so suitable for their purpose,—these model waves cannot be equalled with the pencil, and the magnitude and majesty of the frowning cliffs may never be drawn on canvas to give one a just idea of the reality; here then are subjects to excite the most ambitious.

The Land's End is a notable spot to mariners also, as,—

" The dark Bolerium, seat of storms."

The sea runs here with enormous swells, and from the prominence of the numerous headlands, the tides are irregular; at this western extremity of the coast they are rendered more particularly so on account of the Scilly Islands, which narrow the channel, thus increasing the velocity of the current whether the tide sets to the north or to the south. At an ordinary spring tide the sea rises, at the Land's End, eighteen feet, and from that to twenty-four, according to wind and weather; during storms from the south-west it has risen thirty feet. At the neap tides it rises about thirteen feet ; at a very dead neap it has risen not more than ten feet. During the flood, the tide sets inward from the south for nearly nine hours, the ebb continues only between three and four hours. This peculiarity is extremely dangerous if not known and carefully regarded.

Those who have the least acquaintance with the Land's End, must have heard of the fabled land of Lyonesse, where

> "All day long the noise of battle roll'd
> Among the mountains by the winter sea,
> Till all King Arthur's Table, man by man,"

had fallen

> "Around their lord, King Arthur."

It connected this promontory with the Scilly Isles. The period in which the great inundation occurred overwhelming this tract must have been very remote indeed — long before Phœnician vessels sailed on these waters, long before —

> "Victorious legions, by the Cæsar led,
> Cleaved the rough wave to Britain's hostile shore" —

ages ere the Saxon and the Dane swept like tornadoes over the land. No records have fixed the date ; but the tradition hangs over the sea like a mist which can neither be grasped nor penetrated. We are to believe that it was a fair and beautiful land, rich and fertile, and possessing no less than one hundred and forty churches, all by one terrible convulsion swept away for ever. "Morning had dawned upon as bright a scene as ever met the eye. At evening, there was nought from what was then first termed the Land's End to St. Martin's Head, but a howling and boiling wilderness of waves, bearing here and there upon its bosom a fragment from the perished world beneath, or a corse tossed upon the billows, over which sea-birds wheeled and screamed."

Those who have told the tradition strangely blend distant periods of history together; but in confirmation of the assertion that the land did exist, fishermen, in recent times, are reported to have drawn up portions of doors and windows; and the rocks in the channel which rise above the sea, are said to crown the summits of the hills of the submerged territory. About midway between the Land's End and Scilly are the "Seven Stones" which the Cornish called "Lethas," and the space within the stones "Tregas" a dwelling. There is also a story to support the tradition of the Lyonesse, or Lethowsow, relating to one Trevillian, who swam on horseback to the shore during the inundation, and in memory thereof the family bears for its arms, gules, a horse, argent, issuing out of the sea.

Geologists have written that the Lyonesse existed only in imagination; that from the present natural appearances of the cliffs such a separation of land never happened. Thus is modern science as ruthless as the ocean, and the fond and marvellous stories and traditions of ancient days are swept away; and we are to believe only what we really see and feel.

When the atmosphere is clear, the Scilly Isles, eight leagues distant, may be seen, like misty lines of cirrus clouds, streaking the horizon. Their history is as shadowy as their appearance from this spot. These are the supposed Cassiterides of the ancients, whither the Phœnicians and Greeks came for tin; the Silures of the Romans, who banished to these, then barren isles, offenders to the state; and legends say they were often pounced on by the sea-kings who infested the coasts. But whatever may have been the changes which swept over them in times past, they are now peaceable and flourishing; their appearance is altered only by the course of the seasons or by the varied aspects of calm and storm.

Perhaps there is no period of the year more interesting than the first week in June to visit these islands. It is then that one may calculate on fine weather, and if a fisherman, sport with hook and line, if a naturalist, much amusement may be had in botanical rambles, or in collecting sea-birds and their eggs. This is the time when one need not clamber rocks and precipices in vain for the eggs of the guillemot, razor-bill, puffin, and cormorant. If you are no climber, you may find in the sand, laid with no preparation but a slight depression, four grey spotted eggs with their smaller ends converging — thus occupying the smallest possible space; these probably are the eggs of the ring dottrel. In other places, and generally in the sand or herbage about the shore, may be found the eggs of the different species of tern, including the sandwich, whiskered, gull billed, arctic, roseate and common terns. Of all these the most elegant is the roseate; the whole of the under parts of this bird exhibit, in the spring and summer,

THE ROSEATE TERN.

the most lovely pink hue, sometimes in certain lights, evanescent, whilst in others it has a more powerful glow of colour. The shearwaters breed in long hori-zontal holes in the sand, laying their white, glossy, large egg at the farther extremity. Storm petrels, too, breed in large numbers and in similar places, and there is no difficulty in obtaining their eggs, which are of a light brown towards the larger end. Several other interesting and rare British birds have been captured on the islands. Amongst the birds of prey, the peregrine, kestrel, and merlin falcons, Montagu's harrier, &c. Of the rarer land birds may be mentioned : the hoopoe, generally met with every spring, the rose-coloured pastor, which has been obtained in a very perfect state of plumage. Mr. D. W. Mitchell, the late Secretary to the Zoological Society, during a visit to Scilly obtained one of the rarest of British birds, the pectoral stint. Mr. Yarrell, in his "British Birds," has referred to this capture, and also under the article Manks shearwater, has given a very graphic account of the habits of that bird.

THE OSPREY.

Much attention has been given to the natural history of the Scilly Islands of late years, and a careful observation has been made of the occurrence of the different species of birds, both land and aquatic;

the result is, that these islands can boast of a very
large proportion of British birds, either as resi-
dents, as casual visitors, or birds of passage.   Nearly
all the smaller warbling birds have been observed
there occasionally in the migratory seasons, such as
the willow wren, blackcap, garden warbler, reed
warbler, flycatchers, pied and spotted, and another
very rare British bird, only lately added to the list,
the short-toed lark.   The brown longbeaked snipe
has also been captured on these islands.

Among the birds of prey should have been mentioned the osprey or fishing hawk; this, as well as
most of the other birds referred to, as being met with
at Scilly, has also occasionally visited the western
parts of Cornwall.

The Wolf Rock lies south of the channel betwixt
the Scilly Islands and the Land's End : it is said to
have its name from the peculiar howling noise made
by the waves around it.   As it is a very dangerous
spot for mariners, an attempt was made some years
ago to fix the figure of a wolf in copper on it, so that
the wind would make a loud noise in passing through
it, and ring the bells attached, but the tides were
found so violent, and the waves dashed over the rock
in such a savage manner, that, after two or three
ineffectual attempts, the good-intentioned design was
obliged to be abandoned.   In a work on the Scilly
Islands, published about a hundred years ago, is the
following curious account of the Wolf Rock.

"Some report its howling by the waves or tides
formerly rushing through its cavities, whence it was

called *Wolf*, which noise some pretend was a signal
for mariners to avoid it; but fishermen in those parts
being disturbed at the noise, silenced it by filling up
the vacuity with stones. A person taking a cursory
survey of the channel, in the year 1742, as far as
Scilly, took one of his stations at low water, as he told
me, upon this rock, where he observed a cavity like a
brewer's copper, with rubbish at the bottom, without
being able to assign a cause for its coming there; and
going to make his inquiry, the weather changing of
a sudden, and beginning to blow, the seas beating
over him he could not inform himself, but was towed
off, with his instruments, by a rope, cast from a boat
at a distance. For the better security of shipping
in the channel he proposed to the Trinity Board the
mooring of a buoy to this rock, in such a manner
that it should swing clear of the rock, carrying a bell
upon it so as to ring by the motion of the waves, and
to give notice of danger, but this jingling scheme (of
buoy bells, upon the *English* coast for alarming us)
was not then accepted; on a supposition that the
fishermen (not approving the music) would remove
the bells, when they catched no fish."

Amongst the other numerous objects in sight, is
the Longships Lighthouse. The rock on which it is
built is called Carn Brâs—the great carn—and rises
71 feet above low-water mark, during spring tides.
From the base of the house to the top of the lantern
is 52 feet; and from the top of the lantern to the
top of the bonnet or cowel, which crowns the
structure, is 4 feet; this gives 56 feet for the height

of the lighthouse; including the rock, the total height
is about 127 feet. The circumference of the building
at the base is 68 feet; the wall is 4 feet thick at the
base, 2 feet 7 inches at the top. The entrance, which

THE LONGSHIPS.

faces N.E., is barricaded with two strong doors, perfectly watertight. The house is divided into three
stories, exclusive of the lantern; the lower room is
used for keeping water, coals, and provisions; the
second is a cooking room and oil store; the third a
sleeping room. The lantern is 11 feet 6 inches
diameter within; the height of the glass 7 feet.
19 Argand lamps burn every night, being lit as soon
as the sun sinks beyond the horizon.

Originally, two men only were stationed at the

lighthouse; but it once happened that one of them died; thus the other was alone on the dreary rock. Since that period four men have been employed in the service, three being always in the lighthouse, and one on shore. The exchange is made every twenty-eight days if weather permits. The landing is difficult and dangerous. In winter, when gales prevail, the tide rushes on this rock furiously—preventing the exchange for many weeks beyond the stated time. It is related, that an inspector, who was rather difficult to be pleased, on one of his visitations to the lighthouse, was more than usually inclined to be dissatisfied; in particular, he did not see the necessity of so large a stock of provisions being kept—so near the land, surely they might fetch their store oftener. But whilst he thus employed himself grumbling and finding fault, the wind arose, and the sea began to complain also; the spray soon flew over the rock, and thus did the waves continue to boil and rage for nine weeks, keeping the inspector a prisoner all that time. The men received no orders to alter their arrangements as to provisions.

The lantern of the lighthouse was once broken in during a fearful storm, and on that memorable night, it is said, the hair of one of the keepers changed from jet black to white. One would think that the occupation of light-keeper on such a spot would not be much sought after, yet some men have been engaged on this rock for twenty years. The lighthouse was built in the year 1793 by a Mr. Smith; it was constructed at Sennen Cove previously to its being erected on the rock. It is entirely of granite, a plentiful supply being at hand; the stones are dovetailed one into the other, secured by oak trennels, and strongly cemented.

During rough weather the waves rise over the whole structure and break fathoms above the lantern; but it is almost always clothed in foam and spray, like sheets of driving snow.

Houses for the lightkeepers have lately been built on the brow of the hill over Sennen Cove. The establishment is under the management of the Trinity Board.

On either side of the rock on which the lighthouse stands, are two others: that to the south is called "Tal y mean," the "Tall Rock;" the other, to the north, is called "Meinek," which simply signifies "Strong."

Nearer the shore is a rock, from its peculiar shape, named the Kettle's Bottom.

The rock which stands a few yards from the very extreme point of the promontory is called Careg an Pell, or Peal, the Spire Rock. Tradition says an iron spire was once fixed on the top of it, and that it was thrown down and broken in three pieces during a storm in 1648; its fall was considered a prognostic of some direful event. The following year Charles I., who strongly possessed the sympathy of Cornwall, was beheaded. It was thought by some either to have been erected by the Romans or by Athelstan as a trophy after he conquered the Scilly Islands. "But," as old Hals quaintly observes, "it is not very probable such a piece of iron, in this salt sea and air, without being consumed by rust, could endure so long a time."

Pell is also said to mean " far off," or " most remote." This was the ancient British name for the promontory itself, and from this word Camden thinks it possible that Diodorus derived his Belerium; Ptolemy called it Bolerium. This name was applied to the whole district which it has been the object of these pages to illustrate. It is also said to be named from Bellerius, a Cornish giant;—by the following lines this tradition will ever be remembered:—

> " Or whether thou to our moist vows deny'd
>   Sleep'st by the fable of Bellerus old."

The British bards named it Penrhin Guard, " the Promontory of Blood," from some fearful conflict which took place here; it was also called Penwith, a " promontory to the left;" the hundred still retains the name. The ancient inhabitants, in their language, called it Pen-von-las, " the end of the earth," in which sense it is now termed the Land's End, as being the farthest part of the island westward.

Some rocks on this coast assume the most singular and fantastic forms; in passing around the north side of the promontory one is seen, leaning against a perpendicular mass, which from some fancied resemblance has acquired the name of Dr. Johnson's Head; and it is very curious that the moss and lichens grow more thickly on the top and hinder part, having the appearance of a wig.

DR. JOHNSON'S HEAD.

The various gulls and other sea-birds, hovering and screaming around, call loudly for attention. Several species will be observed, from the large black-backed and glaucous gulls, which are the largest, to the little gull, which is one of the rarest of the family. The lesser black-backed, herring, black-headed, kitti-wake, and common gulls, with razor-bills, guillemots, cormorants, shags, shearwaters, stormy petrels, and gannets, may all be seen following their vocations in diving, soaring, swimming, and screaming, giving life to the scene, yet quite in harmony with the wild and romantic form which nature assumes on these rugged cliffs.

There is a large pond near Sennen, surrounded by a morass, which is considered the best piece of snipe

ground in the district. During hard frost this pond
and marsh attract large quantities of wild fowl.
Some years since a white stork was shot there; it is
now preserved in the Penzance Natural History
Society's Museum. Amongst the rarer wading birds
which have been procured from this locality, are the
green, wood, and dusky sandpipers. A great variety
of ducks have been obtained from here, such as the
shieldrake, gadwall, garganey, longtailed, scaup, and
velvet ducks; specimens of the horned and eared
grebe, and the great plover have also been captured.

THE LITTLE GULL.

CHAP. IV.

From Sennen Church-town a pathway through some fields leads to Sennen Cove and Whitsand Bay. It was from this spot that Athelstan, after his final conflict with the Cornish, started to subdue the Scilly Islands. Stephen landed here on his first arrival in England, and so did Perkin Warbeck with some of his followers, when he sought to seize the crown he claimed. It is also said to have been the landing-place of King John when he returned from Ireland.

The beach is entirely composed of beautiful white sand, from which the bay derives its name, and

WHITSAND BAY.

amongst which rare microscopic shells may be gathered by handfuls; amongst the varieties are *Zonites pygmæus, Limnæus glaber, Conovulus denticulatus*, and in a small stream near by, *Succinea Pfeifferi*.

During low water, at the southern extremity of the beach, the junction of the slate and granite may be distinctly seen; some of the rocks have a curious appearance, one half being dark, the other light, the line of demarcation being as straight as if drawn with a ruler; large veins of granite intersect and traverse the slate in all directions.*

Hillocks of sand, scantily covered with vegetation, rise beyond the beach; a pile of rock on the summit of one is called Cairn Olva, " the Cairn at the head of the beach." Several tracts along the north coast of Cornwall are in this manner overrun with sand, and appear to have been subject to sudden changes. At Vellan-Dreath, on the shores of this bay, an entire

---

* When the rocks are exposed during low water, beautiful varieties of sea-anemones may be found on the Penwith coast: the following is a list of some of the more interesting: —

Actinoloba dianthus,	Anthea cereus,
Sagartia bellis,	Actinia mesembryanthemum,
———— miniata,	———— fragacea,
———— rosea,	Bunodes gemmacea,
———— venusta,	———— Ballii,
———— nivea,	Tealia crassicornis,
———— sphyrodeta,	Corynactis viridis,
———— troglodytes,	Zoanthus Couchii,
———— viduata,	Caryophyllia Smithii,
———— parasitica,	Balanophyllia regia.

skeleton, about the size of a large deer, was found at
the depth of thirty feet; near it was a prostrate oak
tree, twenty feet long and about eighteen inches in
diameter; numerous leaves were on the branches, and
impressions of them were plain on the earth; near by
was a deer's horn two and a half feet long, with the
branched antlers attached. The animal and tree
appeared to have been hurried away and over-
whelmed at the same instant.

As the name implies, Vellan-Dreath is the " mill in
the sand; " nothing, however, of the mill is now to be
seen. In the days of " good Queen Bess " it is well
known that the Spaniards had a particular fondness
for roving around the English coasts, and that in
some few secluded and defenceless places they did
what damage lay in their power. The old miller of
Vellan-Dreath had heard rumours of these would-
be invaders, but did not consider that such matters
concerned him in the least, and went on grinding in
his usual quiet way. Early one summer morning the
miller rose to turn the flushet and let the water on
the wheel. The supply was but scanty, and sometimes he let it run all night. He had accomplished
his object, and was about to enter the mill, when he
happened to look seaward. The sea, as is often the
case here in early mornings, was almost totally obscured by a thick mist, which the sun as yet had not
sufficient power to dispel; however, during a mo-
mentary break in the fog, he imagined he saw
something like the mast of a ship, and before he had
recovered his surprise, he heard the splashing of oars

near the beach just beneath. This sound proceeded
from a boat which had put off from the galley. It
contained five or six well-armed Dons, who soon left
the imprint of their boots on the smooth beach of
sand. The mill was to them an object of attraction.
In the meantime the miller, suspecting how matters
stood, had got within his fortress and determined at
least to make some resistance. His only companion
was his son, a rough and hardy Cornishman. The
door of the mill was a " heps," or hapse, consisting
of an upper and lower part, each opening indepen-
dent of the other; in the upper one was a hole to
admit a finger to lift the catch ; this was used by the
besieged as a loophole, and an old musket was handled
with such advantage that the Spaniards for a time
retired. As an extra force was shortly after seen
approaching to their assistance, the millers thought
it time to save their lives. To cover their retreat
they set fire to a rick of furze which had been collected as fuel; the wind being favourable blew the
smoke into the eyes of the Spaniards, and when they
first saw the millers they were half way up the hill,
each with a sack of flour on his back, which was
excellent protection from the bullets. As bad luck
would have it, however, the old man was struck by
a stray shot : dropping his load, he for the time
escaped, but did not recover from the injury. When
the son was in safety he threw down the sack, pro-
testing that it was some pounds heavier than when
he started, on account of the lead lodged in it.

The Spaniards in their rage demolished the mill, but did not proceed farther into the country.

Some years ago a curious key supposed to have belonged to the mill, was found near the spot, and the mill stone was for a long time to be seen placed before a blacksmith's shop at Sennen.

Such is the Legend of the Mill.

The bay is bounded on the north by Cape Cornwall. The Brisons, two fearful rocks south of the Cape, are conspicuous objects: from this spot they look like one rock, but we shall see them differently from another part of the coast.

At Sennen Cove is a coast-guard station and several fishermen's cottages; seine boats are kept here, and considerable quantities of fish caught. The seine fishery is carried on chiefly in sandy bays such as this. As soon as fish are perceived near the shore, the seine boat, propelled by oars, proceeds to the spot; the net, about 220 fathoms in length and 12 fathoms deep, is dropped across the course of the fish, so as to enclose them in a circle. Whilst two boats are engaged in bringing the ends of the net together, another is stationed near the opening — the men dashing the water with oars and loaded ropes to frighten the fish back. When the seine is closed, and a great number of fish found to be within, or if the tide runs strong, the net is moored by heavy grapnels — the upper part being buoyed by cork. Towards evening, when the tide recedes, a boat with a smaller net, called the tuck net, enters within the circle to take up some of the fish — the men splashing the water as before. When the fish are raised to the surface, they make such a noise beating the water, that the voices of the men can scarcely be heard; they are then taken from the net to the boat in baskets. If there is a very large catch, all the fish cannot be taken up at once, but they may remain secured within the seine for several days. Should rough weather suddenly come on when they are thus situated, there is great loss: this, however, does not often occur, for the fishermen are so well acquainted with the appearances of sea and sky which precede a storm, that if there is danger the fish are landed as rapidly as possible.

The Great Weever, a curious fish which burrows in the sand, is sometimes brought up in the tuck net; it is most brilliantly coloured, and has the peculiarity of a long sharp spine on each side of the head, and if incautiously handled, it strikes with these weapons an unerring blow; a puncture from these spines is poisonous, it causes great pain, which rapidly extends from the hand to the shoulder — the injured part swells very much, and turns to a livid purple colour.

Strange marks are sometimes seen along the sand by the margin of the waves, which might puzzle any one who did not know that the launce or sand-eel burrows here, the marks being made by men pricking for them. The launce swims about the shore during the day, and burrows in the sand by night. They are caught by scraping in the sand with a pole to which an iron crook is attached, and must be pulled up with a sudden jerk and rapidly secured, or they again hide themselves. Moonlight nights are selected for this purpose.

Among other things for which the Land's End is celebrated, is the Land's End Pollack. Under this title, however, two species are included, the Whiting Pollack, *Merlangus Pollachius*, the Lythe of Scotland, and the Rauning Pollack, *M. carbonarius*, called in the North a Coalfish. These fish are here to be found in perfection and of enormous size, when compared with those captured elsewhere. The Whiting Pollack is generally preferred for the table,

THE WHITING POLLACK.

but the other is better than most fish. These two kinds are easily distinguished from each other. The Rauning, or as it might now be written Ravening, Pollack is very dark or black, and the line which runs along its side from the head to the tail is straight, or very nearly so, whilst in the Whiting Pollack, of which a figure is given, this line is a

graceful curve. Both these fish like strong tides and
a rocky shore, and love to linger in the wake of some
rock along which a current is rushing; with their
head to the tide they watch a passing prey, and dart
on it with great rapidity. During summer, the
young of the Whiting Pollack come in shoals into
our bays and harbours and sport about, rippling the
surface as they rise to the flies or any floating bait.
The Rauning Pollack is a deep water species, and
rarely comes near the shore.

At Sennen Cove was an ancient chapel, called by
the people Chapel Idné, the "narrow chapel;" being
forty-five feet long and fifteen feet wide. It is now
converted into a dwelling. Tradition says it was
founded by one Lord of Goonhilly, who possessed
some portion of the land of Lyonesse. There was a
holy well of some repute here also.

Three rocks stretching away one after the other
from the shore are known by the names of Cowloe,
Bo Cowloe, and Little Bo. The word Cowloe is
probably from Cowlas—the "bay with a building,"
the chapel being once a solitary structure here.

Before leaving the spot we notice *Galium Vail-
lantii* growing about the walls by the fishermen's
cottages. The following algæ may be gathered in
this locality—*Grateloupia filicina, Kallymenia reni-
formis* and *Dubyi, Nitophyllum Hilliæ, N. Bonne-
maisonii,* and *N. Gmelini, Rytiphlœa complanata,*
and *Polysiphonia pulvinata.*

It is a steep ascent to Pedn-mên-du, the " head-

land of black rock," which forms the western boundary of Whitsand Bay.   Its height is about 140 feet;
the northern part is composed of immense perpendicular masses of granite; on the southern side the
rocks are rugged and waterworn, and split into small
quadrangular masses.   On the summit is a flag-staff
belonging to the preventive station.   Beneath, just
off the shore, westward of the point, is seen towering
above the waves a rock of a peculiar and pleasing
form; it is known as the Irish Lady.   The legend is,
that a wreck having happened there, of all the souls
that were on board only a lady was seen, clinging to
this rock.   It was found that the ship belonged to
Ireland.   It is suggested also that the rock derives
its name from its graceful form, for by the aid of a
little imagination, it may appear to the spectator not
unlike a lady in a long black robe advancing into
the sea.

The fishermen of the locality say that the ghost of
the drowned lady, with a rose in her mouth, is still
often seen on the rock.   Fishermen are very superstitious—and though frequently at sea by night, and
fearlessly braving the most terrible storms—yet they
have a dread of walking about the land at night,
especially along the shore where wrecks have happened; the ghosts of the drowned they believe to
haunt these spots.   There is a superstition connected
with the coast, that when a person is drowned, his
voice may afterwards be heard during storms " hailing
his own name," and a legend has been told in verse

THE IRISH LADY.

of a girl, whose lover had thus perished, watching on
the headlands to hear this dread sound —

> "Her gaze is where the weltering waves
> Thunder along the trembling strand;
> She heeds not how the mad storm raves,
> Her lover's voice comes to the land."

Still further from the shore, marked by a line of
white foam, is the "Shark's Fin."

As we proceed hence to Maen Castle, the Land's
End appears to great advantage, stern and wild; the
cavern, previously alluded to, is now seen as an open
archway through the headland. Maen Castle was
merely a rude work of loose stones across a piece of
projecting land; structures of this kind and so
situated are called "Cliff Castles." At Cairn-mên-
ellas, close by, are the remains of a "kist-vaen,"* and
some rocks arranged in a singular manner, which
have been considered Druidical.

After passing Cairn Clog — the "cairn of hard
rock," and crossing Hal-hagar, the "ugly moor," we
arrive again at the Land's End. In looking back it
will be seen that this point and Pedn-mên-du form
the extremities of a bay, to which the name of
Gamper is given.

The line of coast from Sennen Cove to the Land's
End will be found of much geological interest, especially from the frequent occurrence of rounded and
waterworn masses of stone, of various sizes, and in
situations where they could not have been originally

---

* See page 17.

placed. At the southern termination of Pedn-mên-du some straggling boulders rest on the granite about thirty feet above the sea; they will be met with again at Gamper Hole, near Maen Castle, a cavern whose walls are solid granite, the boulders connected with gravelly clay forming an arched roof, the lowest being forty feet above high-water mark. Indeed, they are found in all the numerous caverns which open from the face of these cliffs. The roof of that next the Land's End is an entire mass of boulders, as round as possible, with gravel and clay in the interstices, and in the very centre of the cavern called the Land's End Hole, is a mass of boulders and pebbles from thirty to forty feet above the highest tide.

These caverns are dark, gloomy recesses, some of them running into the land for 100 feet, the floors of the greater number being washed by the sea, except at low water. They are difficult and dangerous to be got at by persons unacquainted with the locality, yet they will amply repay for the trouble taken to inspect them: the stones rendered slippery by sea-weed must be carefully walked over; the great boulders in the roof look as if they were ready to fall every moment, and one feels as if he were treading on ground which is not under man's dominion—but the sole territory of the wild waves, and the haunts of screaming sea-birds.

The action of the sea is supposed to have made these cavities by wearing away the different softer substances which formerly occupied the space.

The carriage road from the Land's End to the Logan Rock is about four miles in length; there is nothing of particular interest by the way, but by skirting the coast some of the finest cliff scenery of the kingdom is passed. This will make the walk full six miles; there are many ups and downs, hills and valleys to be got over; but the fatigue of the journey is forgotten as the varied and magnificent scenes rise one after the other. Stunted furze spreads over the ground, thickly interwoven with the parasitical dodder, *Cuscuta Epithymum*. Various heaths are also intermixed, presenting altogether gorgeous masses of gold, red, purple, and green, covering acres of land, and clothing whole hill sides in the most brilliant manner.

The engraving represents the heaths so plentifully found in the district, *Erica tetralix*, and *Erica cinerea*, and *Calluna vulgaris*, which generally accompanies them. The Cornish heath, *Erica vagans*, is not met with in this extreme western part of the county; though it is very plentiful at the Lizard, and on Connor Down, near Hayle.

On the ground may be seen also *Lecidea Salweii* and *Borrera leucomela*. *Borrera flavicans* grows on thorns and apple trees in the district; many specimens with fructification called "shields" have been gathered, twenty or thirty shields being sometimes found on a single tuft; few British specimens in that condition have been gathered elsewhere.

The shore, where it may be approached, affords good Algæ, as *Dasya arbuscula*.

ERICA TETRALIX, E. CINEREA, AND CALLUNA VULGARIS.

Leaving the Land's End, Cairn Creis is seen rising
above the cliff. The Dollar or Dollah rock stands
isolated from the shore, and seems to be a favourite
spot with gulls, as large numbers are generally seen
there congregated. Cairn Creis presents a singular
arrangement of rock, large masses project and hang
over as if the gentlest touch would send them bound-

ing into the boiling surge beneath. Near this spot a
windlass is fixed on the edge of a precipice perhaps
a hundred feet deep, and is used for drawing up
sea-weed. In this indentation of the coast is Greeb
Zawn; the latter word will frequently occur, and
signifies a "hole in the cliff through which the sea
passes."

That grand pile of rock, entirely surrounded by
sea, called in Cornish "An Marogeth Arvowed," the
Armed Knight, has for some time been in view; from

THE ARMED KNIGHT.

here is seen its peculiar form, from which the name
is derived; on the summit the rock assumes the
shape of a man's head, in profile; the portion which

forms the breast looks not unlike armour, so regularly is the granite jointed. Its height may be 200
feet. It was also called Guela or Guelaz, the "rock
easily seen."

The next headland is Cairn Greeb, the "Cairn like
a cock's comb." Enys Dodnan, "the island with

ENYS DODNAN.

soil upon it," now appears; a cavern about forty feet
high goes completely through it; another does not
penetrate so far; the perpendicular quartz veins
above them may be distinctly seen from the shore.
The island has been reached, without the aid of a
boat, during very low tides, but it is a venturesome
undertaking. In the accompanying illustration
the south side of the Armed Knight is seen between
the land and the Enys; in the distance, on the left,
is the Longships lighthouse.

On the land opposite the island is Cairn Enys, and

near by Cairn Tork, "rocks like loaves;" another
fantastic stone is called the Ape's Head.   By change
of light or the position of the spectator, the rocks
in this locality may be made to assume gro-
tesque and monstrous forms, especially when the
sun is low, and the masses of rock in shade stand
out distinctly against the sky; then appear huge
heads, great crouching lions, and other terrible
shapes, that—

> " like giants stand
> To sentinel enchanted land "

—rendered still more mysterious by the lengthened
shadows of the hills and the haze from the sea at
sunset.

Passing the Cove called Zawn Wells, and the site
of the old signal house, we come on Pordenack, "very
hilly," Point *; in some respects the most remarkable
of all the headlands along the coast; it is by far the
finest cliff we have yet noticed, and is only equalled
by one other, Tol-pedn, not yet reached.   It rises
about 200 feet perpendicularly from the sea, and
appears as if composed of a series of columns constructed of huge cubical blocks, bearing a great
resemblance to basaltic pillars (though far larger),
not only in their prismatic form, but in the apparent
regularity of their sides and division into joints.   On
the summit of one of the crags, a rock about five feet
high is very delicately poised, and appears to be
resting on a mere point; it is the most striking object

---

* Turner was much impressed with the grandeur of this headland,
and made a drawing of it.

of the range. Fearful as it may seem, lads of the neighbourhood do not hesitate to stand on the top of it. Finer veins of granite, of a reddish colour, inter-

PORDENACK POINT.

sect the perpendicular cliff from top to bottom, one about four feet wide is particularly straight and regular.

Cairn Vean, the "Little Cairn," Cairn Sperm, the "Cairn of Thorns," and Cairn Voel, the "Bleak Cairn," follow in succession. Lion's Den, beneath, is a large cavern. Several years ago a vessel was driven right into it, and of a crew of twenty-five only four were saved; two were found locked in each other's arms, and were said to have been friends who had passed through many dangers together; during the war they had been imprisoned in France, and in company effected their escape. As they were found, so were

they laid together beneath the turf on the cliff.
One poor fellow was discovered beneath a great
boulder, which the efforts of several men could not
move, but which the sea in its violence had rattled
about as a mere pebble. Portions of the wreck were
floated into Nanjizel, close by, and the boom of the
vessel was thrown up and lodged, standing on its
end, on a ledge in the face of the cliff, thirty feet
above high-water mark.

Cairn Evall is one of the principal spots where

CAIRN EVALL.

the prismatic and cubical forms of the granite are
seen united. The engraving shows the southern side.

Some little creeks along here are called Môz rang,

the " Maid's Pool ;" Pludn, the " Pool ;" and Polgrean
the " Green Pool;" then we arrive at Cairn Cravah, and
Zawn Reeth, the " Red Cavern," the soil here being of
that colour. A narrow ridge projects into the sea from
this hollow, and is known as " the horse." We are
now fairly within Mill Bay or Nanjizel, " the cove
beneath the vale." This spot has somewhere been
spoken of under the name of " the Song of the Sea,"
perhaps the waves were thought to make a singing
noise : no tradition of such a name is remembered in
the locality. Cairn les Boel, the " cairn of the bleak
place," pierced by a cavern, forms the southern
boundary of the cove. The cavern is called Zawn
Pyg, " cave like a bird's beak." The beach is composed of beautiful white sand, chiefly fragments and
particles of shells, of which many unbroken specimens
may be gathered, similar to those at Whitsand Bay.

Nanjizel is one of the most picturesque and romantic coves on the coast. A little stream, dividing
the parishes of Sennen and St. Levan, comes down
the valley and dashes over the rocks very prettily;
it passes through a natural archway, just before
spreading peaceably on the sand. Another tall archway composed of soil and rock, stands below, isolated
and unconnected with the side of the cliff. The sea
is continually fretting them away, and some day,
most probably, they will come down with a thundering noise.

The rugged rock south of Cairn les Boel is Bosistow
Island, on which numerous gulls, cormorants, and
other sea birds build. Gaining the summit of the

NANJIZEL.

acclivity we pass along the edge of Bosistow cliff and enter Pendower, "the head of the water," Cove. The green turf slopes down pleasantly towards the

NATURAL ARCHWAY, NANJIZEL.

sea, and standing on the highest part is a very excellent Logan Rock. It was discovered to possess the quality of "logging" accidentally, by a man who was employed in watching the coast for the lord of the manor. A vessel had been wrecked in the cove immediately below, and whilst engaged in his duty, he leaned against a mass of rock, which, to his astonishment he found in motion; the oscillation having been produced by the force of the wind. This stone is in the form of an irregular parallelopiped for somewhat more than half its length, and then it slopes away in a wedge-like shape to its north-east angle.   The

BOSISTOW LOGAN ROCK.

length of the longest side is about fifteen feet, and its thickest end about twenty feet in circumference. At a rough calculation, allowing for the irregularities of the surface, it may be computed to contain about three hundred cubic feet, and to weigh about twenty tons.   It is very easily set in motion.   I have seen it "logged" by the wind.   Rocking stones frequently occur amongst the tabular and cubiform masses of granite in this district, but they only attract attention when of considerable magnitude.

There is a large cavern in the cliff here, but it is inaccessible from the land.   Another cavity is called

Zawn Kellys, the "fallen cavern." Cairn Barra, at
the southern extremity of the cove, projects considerably into the sea. From this place to Tol-pedn
magnificent examples of rock scenery are passed; the
names of some of the most notable points are Cairn
Mellyn, the " Yellow Cairn ; " Pellitrass Point, Pellow
Zawn, Porthloe, and Cairn bras en guethen bras, the
" Great Cairn."

Conspicuous objects on the high ground above Tol-
pedn, are two land-marks or beacons; one is painted
red, the other black and white ; they are about twelve
feet high, and are placed in a line with a dangerous
rock called the Runnel Stone, which lies about a mile
from the shore, and has been fatal to many vessels,
as it is sometimes totally covered by the sea, and they
run on it unawares.

Looking seaward from the beacons, Tol-pedn,
" the holed headland," lies a little to the right. The
descent over the turf, which is beautifully even and
smooth, is very steep and slippery ; we must go down
cautiously, for a false step may roll us over the rocks
and into the sea far beneath. We shall have to
walk very near the edge of the great yawning chasm,
called the "Funnel." It is but six or seven feet
from the verge of the cliff, and descends perpendicularly. At the bottom, a cavern from the face of
the cliff meets it, the two cavities making a letter L;
the opening on the surface was formed by the falling
in of the roof of a cavern similar to the many others
previously noticed.

When the tide recedes, the cavern may be entered,

after getting down the shelving cliff, a difficult task
to many, but when accomplished we are amply repaid

THE FUNNEL.

for the labour, by the magnificent sight of the cliffs.
It is impossible to imagine anything finer in coast
scenery; near the entrance to the cavern rises a
perpendicular wall of granite to the height of 200
feet, with scarcely a crack or fissure on its surface—
a solid, impenetrable mass.   Were all our coasts like
this, Britannia would truly need

> " no bulwarks,
> No towers along the steep."

For it has defied the Atlantic for ages—and mocks
the power of man; a few of the waves which roll in
here would shiver the noblest architectural work to
pieces, whilst they may beat for ever on this living

CHAIR LADDER, TOL-PEDN-PENWITH.

rock, and it remains changeless and unharmed. But the finest pile of granite in the county is on the left, named Chair Ladder: the whole mass appears as if built up of great cubical blocks, reared one on the other.

During a dark and foggy night, a few years ago, a steamer ran against this cliff. It is said that the crew imagined they had passed the Land's End and were steering up the North Channel. Her dangerous position was discovered when too late, indeed, she was so near the cliff, that one of the sailors got on the bowsprit and sprang on a ledge of rock at the base, and though it scarcely seems credible, he managed to reach the summit. Had it been light enough for him to have seen his perilous situation he would not have attempted to scale the cliff at such a fearful spot. The steamer was soon a total wreck; but the remainder of the crew took to a boat; and as the weather was not particularly rough, they arrived safely in Mount's Bay.

Let us inspect the cavern. The entrance is strewn with huge boulders, worn round and smooth, some of them several tons weight; playthings for the waves. The cave extends nearly 150 feet, the floor rising so rapidly that the extremity is probably fifty feet above the mouth. We now look up the Funnel and see the blue sky, and the fleecy clouds passing by, seeming higher than ever through this great tube. It is an awfully strange place. The walls are damp with trickling moisture; bright emerald mosses are sparkling in dark crevices, and graceful ferns festoon

the numerous rents and fissures, softening the rigid
surfaces of the rock.   The monotony is broken occasionally by the wild scream of a gull or the chatter
of a chough.

AT CHAIR LADDER.

The red-legged crow, or Cornish chough, for a
long period selected the Funnel Rock as a secure and
inaccessible place for its nest.   It is now, however,

rarely seen on the coast, though at one time very plentiful. The egg of this bird is much sought after by collectors : it is of a pale grey wood brown with obscure brown spots, and is rather larger than the egg of the jackdaw.

But the waves without appear to be getting louder and to be rushing more violently to the opening : it is time to hasten away, lest we be shut in. Some time ago, two gentlemen from the eastern part of the kingdom entered the cavern without being acquainted with the tides, and having lingered too long within, when they came to the entrance the sea had formed a barrier to the ledge on the opposite side which it was necessary to gain. It was truly an awful situation, for the mere sight of such a place is enough to appal a stranger to the coast, much more to be so uncomfortably imprisoned. Fortunately, one of them could swim, and managed to get across, and hastened to the nearest dwelling for assistance to his luckless companion, whose position was certainly not an enviable one during the absence of his friend. To botanise, or meditate pleasantly on geology was impossible ; but for a long half hour must he consider the chances of escape—will the waves come in and carry him away ?—has his friend safely reached the summit of the cliff?—are there any dwellings in the neighbourhood, and can assistance be procured?—how to be got out, dragged through the surge, or drawn up like a bucket through the Funnel ? After remaining in this state of suspense and terror for some time, a welcome shout is heard above,— his friend has returned with some fishermen, who, by the use of ropes, draw him safely to the summit.

Subsequently to this event, a more dangerous adventure happened to a gentleman of the county, the particulars of which he related to me himself. He had agreed to meet a friend, who was staying at the village of Treryn, for the purpose of sketching the surrounding scenery, on a certain day at Tolpedn. On arriving there he found that his friend had not come. As the morning had been cloudy and threatened rain, the sketcher thought the gentleman would not have started from Penzance. "As I was on the spot I was unwilling to lose the day, and determined to go into the cave. Near the base of the cliff is a ledge of rock, from which you have to drop down to the beach: this is sometimes accomplished by being lowered by a rope—a strong fellow holding the rope and another holding on to him behind. This practice is observed by the guides, but persons often go down without such assistance. I had been there before with my friend, but he, considering it dangerous, refused to assist me to descend. Being now alone I thought I would attempt it, but found I could not drop from the ledge; descending to another point I made up my mind to swim for the opening. I prepared accordingly, and got in the surf; struggled towards the mouth of the cave, which I reached, and grasped a huge boulder, when the undertow of the waves took me back suddenly for some yards, plunging my head violently under water. Recovering, I made another attempt, and again failed; the rocks being

ENTRANCE TO THE CAVERN, TOL-PEDN.

covered with slimy sea-weed gave me no hold. I then swam back to the ledge from which I had started, caught hold of it to rest myself and to determine on further proceedings. Deciding to make a rapid swim with the waves, not giving them time to recede until I was stranded, I ventured forth again, and was hurried violently in; the sea-weed was still a formidable impediment, but I managed to get on the floor of the cave, which I examined, gathered a fern, *Asplenium marinum,* held it in my mouth and swam back." Reflections on this exploit to those who know the spot would be useless, and cautions to visitors equally so, as not many will be likely to imitate it.

A large metalliferous vein crosses this cavern from east to west, some parts of which being of a green colour are supposed to contain copper. In the granite veins of the headland, the felspar will be noticed as of a deep red colour, resembling somewhat the granite of Egypt. In addition to this variety of colour, the rocks are thickly spread with lichens and moss; yellow, orange, and green are beautifully blended. Indeed, if an artist were to paint it as it appears, it might be thought he had daubed his picture with all the colours of his palette merely for a gay effect. A very rare lichen found here is *Lecanora aipospila,* and thickly interwoven with the turf are the golden flowers of the *Lotus hispidus.* The Maiden-hair fern, *Adiantum Capillus-Veneris,* is also said to grow in this locality. It may be obtained with more

certainty between Lelant and St. Ives, though far
less plentiful there than it was a few years back.

On the eastern side of the headland is another
cavern, open from the summit to near the base of
the cliff, where a long narrow channel, covered with

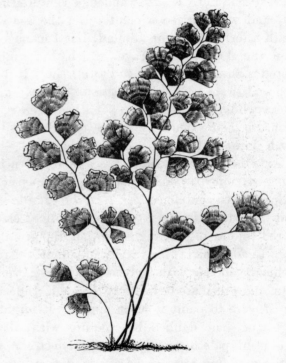

THE MAIDEN-HAIR FERN.

loose rocks, communicates with the sea, which rushes
up, thundering and resounding fearfully as it breaks
within the hollow. The outer edges of the cavern,

formed in the soil, are fretted away, and seem dangerous to approach.

A cliff castle also extended across this headland, but little of it is now to be seen.

The waters off Tol-pedn-penwith are deep, and during the autumn and winter months, boisterous; with nothing but open sea around, the shores are frequently visited by some of the rarer inhabitants of other climes. The white shark of the West Indies occasionally crosses over and pays us a visit in its summer tour; and fish from the Mediterranean, or at least Mediterranean species, are also not unfrequently caught. During the pilchard season in the summer we have the bonito plaice, and the tunny of all sizes in abundance. The only British specimen of the derbio, of which a figure is given, was captured

THE DERBIO.

here, and is now preserved in a private collection at Penzance. Off the Runnel Stone, the boar fish, *Zeus Aper*, though an exceedingly rare British fish, is

abundant; but does not wander far.   As many as a
hundred and ninety-eight specimens have been taken
here in a single day by an ordinary trawler.

Hella, the Fairies' Point, and Polostoc, the "cap-
like headland," are situated between Tol-pedn and
Porthgwarra, the "higher port," a picturesque fishing
cove.   Two tunnels are here cut through the rock to

PORTHGWARRA.

give access to the sand and sea-weed on the beach.
The rocks east of the archways look as if artificially
built up, and exhibit one of the finest veins of red

granite. As at Penberth, the slope to the beach is paved with large stones; on the summit of the ascent, which is very steep, is a windlass to draw up the boats.

Leaving Cairn Scathe, the "boat cairn," and the elevated ground called the Balkin Hill, we arrive at Pol-ledan, the "broad pool," where the cliffs descend so abruptly, that it is impossible to get down to the beautiful beach of sand. Cairn Vassack, the "outside rock," projects from the eastern point of this creek.

From Tol-pedn we have had lovely short turf to walk on, or to sit on if fatigued; and pleasant it is to repose on these verdant spots by the sea, to watch the vessels passing, and the waves coming on the shore, and the reflected lights of the white clouds as they float by; there is nothing to disturb your rest or your meditations, the only sound is from the sea, which " cannot rest," or the plaintive note of some sea bird as it soars along the coast.

Now again we enter on a patch of stunted furze and heath, glad to follow a sheep track when it presents itself.

Standing on some elevated rocks on Porthchapel Point, the remains of St. Levan's Well are seen in a little glen beneath. Still no sign of life—a deep solitude hangs around the great cliffs; the babbling of a little stream over its rough bed, blended with the murmurs of the waves below, is the only sound that breaks on the ear. This was the spot chosen by St. Levan for his chapel or hermitage, which stood on the verge of the cliff; the well was farther back, but steps communicated from one to the

other; these, however, have disappeared. The site
of the chapel can only be guessed at, whilst the
walls of the little baptistery are wildly overgrown
by rushes and tall water plants. Thus is the altar
overthrown, the shrine deserted, and the holy place
become a wilderness.

ST. LEVAN'S WELL.

Tradition says that St. Levan spent some of his
time at Bodillan, about three quarters of a mile
distant; and the path thence through Rosepletha
which he took to go to Pedn-mên-an-mere, the " stone

headland by the sea," to fish, is said to be still visible,
being marked by a stronger vegetation. It is also
said of him, as of St. Neot (probably the persons are
confounded), that he caught only one fish a day,
which served for his sustenance. Whilst thus dwelling in seclusion, he is surprised by an unexpected
visit from his sister and her child. To entertain
them, he proceeds to his fishing station, throws out
the line, and presently draws up a fish, a chad; as he
had visitors, this was not considered dainty enough :
so it is thrown back into the water again. A
second time is the line cast forth, and behold, the
same fish is caught. It is again thrown into the
sea. And now the saint changed his position to
another rock, and threw the line still farther out.
Lo ! what is his surprise when the same fish
again presents itself. Then the saint thought the
hand of Providence was concerned in the matter,
and he bare his catch away. It is cooked, and
placed before the guests, but sad to relate, the
child was choked by the first mouthful. Then was
the holy man much grieved, and repented that
he had given way to the temptation of the fish,
which, he now doubted not, was possessed by an evil
spirit; yet he believed if he had been content with
it at the first time, the melancholy accident would
not have happened, but that it was a punishment
for his dissatisfaction in not accepting gratefully
what Providence had appointed him. From that time
the fishermen of the locality have called the chad
" chuck-cheeld," i. e. choke-child.

St. Levan Church, though not seen from the well, is but a furlong distant; it is in a very sequestered spot, and hidden by the high land which rises toward the sea. The churchyard may be entered freely; there is no iron gate with bolts and locks to keep the people out, or to prevent friends from

ST. LEVAN CHURCH.

visiting the tombs of the " departed"; you may walk on the grass-grown pathways, and read the quaint inscriptions on the stones at your leisure. The grass is so long that the mounds of the graves can scarcely be traced; and the ground near the eastern end of the church is nearly on a level with the walls, being separated by a pathway which runs round the building. It appears as if the earth had been thrown out when the foundation was formed for the church, and so allowed to remain. This rising of the ground close to the walls of old churches is to be observed elsewhere; whether it was an ancient custom, or the result of some superstition, we leave for the consideration of antiquaries; it is, however, very evident that it is not caused at St. Levan, as some suppose it is at other places, by the frequent interment of bodies.

Near the porch is a fine old cross; another stands by the stile at the northern entrance.

The stoup, within the porch, near the handle of the door, is very simple; its only ornamental features are three arches traced on the projecting part. On opening the door, the first object which strikes the eye is a piece of carving close to the door-frame, representing two jesters or clowns. " The jester or fool *in* a church is symbolic of the sectarian heretic, or scoffer at the mysteries, doctrines, or ritual of the Sanctuary. Psalm xxxv., v. 16, ' Subsannaverunt subsannatione.' " *

Descending a step or two to the floor the visitor finds himself in a damp, neglected, and dilapidated church. It is very quaint, and has an appearance of great age; the roof is low, and the bosses on the beams were gilt; a screen of carved panels separates the chancel from the nave, but much of the work is hidden by pews subsequently placed against them.

* R. S. H.

Enough, however, is seen to show the character of the designs, which might afford examples for church restorers and decorators of the present time. On shields are carvings symbolical of the Passion. One

IN ST. LEVAN CHURCH.

bears the cross, with the crown of thorns attached; on another is a hammer; the nails, the spear, &c.,

on others. On one shield is the letter A, and on
another O, these are near the extremity of either end
of the screen, and probably stand for Alpha and
Omega. The accompanying monogram
is frequently repeated, and has been
taken for the initial letters of "Jesus
Hominum Salvator," the three first
letters of Our Saviour's Greek name,
IHSOUS.*

There are many curious carvings also on the bench
ends, in the western part of the church. On one is
a pilgrim monk, with a breviary and a discipline;
on another, is a figure intended to represent the
vesture of our Lord, with a trine detail. Animals
like winged cats and winged bulls, two-headed
eagles, fish, and one with three heads, first of a bird,
then a dragon, then a man, may also be observed.

The north transept is Early English, circa 1220;
the font, perhaps, of the same date. There is only
one mural monument in the church, and that is to
the memory of a Miss Dennis, the daughter of a
farmer who resided in the neighbourhood. By her
own exertions, she became well acquainted with
Latin and Greek; spoke French fluently, and published a novel entitled "Sophia St. Clare;" she is
also said to have written some excellent poetical
compositions.

Amongst the lumber in the belfry are the broken
fragments of the lettered board which the unfor-
tunate Charles ordered to be set up here, as well as

* R. S. H.

in other Cornish churches, expressing his royal thanks for their loyalty and devotion.

The Cornish have ever been noted for their loyalty, and fought valiantly for the king in this cause. Much would it have grieved the worthy cavaliers of those days had they foreseen how this signal mark of royal favour would be cast aside and trampled under foot, even within the sacred walls of a church. The inscription, in its present position, certainly does not comply with Charles's request, — " to perpetuate to all time " the merits of the Cornish.

The King's letter of thanks is as follows :

" Carolus Rex.

" To ye inhabitants of ye county of Cornwall.

" We are so highly sensible of ye extraordinary merits of our county of Cornwall, of their zeal for our Crown, and for ye defence of our person, in a time when We could contribute so little to our own defence, or to their assistance : in a time when not only no reward appeared, but great and probable dangers were threatened to obedience and loyalty : of their great and eminent courage and patience in their indefatigable prosecution of their great work, against so potent an enemy, backed with so strong, rich, and populous cities, and so plentifully furnished and supplied with men, arms, money, ammunition, and provisions of all kinds : and of ye wonderful success with which it pleased Almighty God (though with ye loss of some eminent persons, who shall never be forgotten by Us), to reward their loyalty and patience by many strange victories over their and our enemies, in despite of all human probability and all imaginable disadvantages: that as We cannot be forgetful of so great desert, so We cannot but desire to publish it to all ye world, and to perpetuate to all time ye memory of their merits, and of our acceptance of ye same; and to that end We do hereby render our Royal thanks to that our county, in ye most public and lasting manner We can devise, commanding copies thereof to be printed and published, and one of them to be read in every church and chapel therein, and to be kept for ever as a record of ye same; that as long as ye history of these times and of this nation shall continue, ye memory of how much that county hath merited from Us and our Crown, may be derived with it to posterity.

"Given at our camp of Sudeley Castle, ye 10th day of September, 1643."

There are two bells in the tower, one is dated 1641, the other has the founder's mark, a bell with the letters A. R., date 1754, and the names of the two churchwardens.

Near the cross by the porch which has been alluded to, is a large granite rock, with a rent running through it about a foot wide; but when it is capacious enough for a donkey with a pair of panniers to pass through, then will be the end of all things; such is the popular belief.

Leaving this quiet and interesting spot, we may either descend again to the coast, passing Pedn-mên-an-mere, the Carracks, "rocks," off the headland, and Meinek, "stony," Point, an extremely pleasant walk, and free from furze or bog, or follow the path-way fields from the church, noticing a cross by the way, through Rosepletha farm, and down over the hill to Porthkernou*, commonly called Porcurnow. The beach here is entirely of sand, composed of comminuted shells of the most delicate and beauti-ful structure, and is left so smooth by the waves, that it is almost a pity to make footprints there. Al-though a vast portion of the sand consists of broken pieces, yet a great variety of shells in a perfect state may be collected, belonging to species which are highly prized by conchologists for their rarity.

Observe how the waves come in, with the wind blowing back their crests of foam, like the streaming banners of an army. What splendid curves they form ; what a beautiful transparent emerald is seen as they rise, and how the strand trembles when they fall. The sea does not break here in short fierce waves

"As if contending in their watery chase ;"

but rolls in mighty billows at steady intervals. Even in calm weather the motion of the water is not

---

* "The port surrounded by hornlike hills." Most probably it should be interpreted, "The port of Cornwall," Kernou being the Celtic word for Cornwall.

shown in ripples, but by long swells upheaving its
surface.

Here the works of nature are on the grandest
scale. The rock scenery surrounding the cove cannot be surpassed; to the east, stretching far out, is
Treryn Castle, a noble and wonderful pile. Perhaps
this magnificent scene is best viewed from the sea,
about half a mile from the beach.

The bay off Porthkernou, from its sandy bottom,
abounds in fish of all descriptions, but especially
in flat fish. The turbot, during the summer and
autumnal months, is abundant, and attains a very
large size, as do most of the others. The Halibut

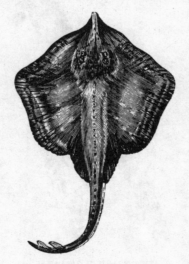

PAINTED RAY (*Raia microcellata*).

has been known to weigh 128 pounds. The skates
and rays are also very fine; some of the rarest

of the British species are found here; a specimen of
the sting ray, *Raia Pastinaca,* was taken a few years
ago, and several specimens of the painted ray have
been captured here; indeed, in this locality it does
not seem rare, as six of them were taken in two
days when specially sought after. The scabbard fish,
Lepidopus argyreus, has on two or three occasions
being taken here, and during the mackerel season
the blackfish of Gesner, *Coryphæna Pompilus,* is
not of rare occurrence.

THE BEARDED TITMOUSE.

A rivulet finds its way into the sea at this cove,
whence a narrow valley extends to some distance. Such

localities are fruitful to the botanist and naturalist.
Rare birds occasionally make their appearance in
this parish; at Rosekestal, about half a mile from
the church, a nearly adult specimen of one of the
most elegant of our native herons, the squacco heron,
was captured; it is remarkable for its diminutive
size and splendid plumage, which, when complete, is
adorned with light flowing plumes from the head and
back. The annexed illustration represents one of
our smaller tits, the bearded titmouse. For elegance
and gracefulness of form nothing can exceed the
beauty of this little bird. It is of very rare occurrence in Cornwall, though frequently seen in the
extensive marshes on the Thames. The specimen
from which the engraving was made was obtained
in a sedgy bottom near St. Levan Church; it is a
male bird in a perfect state of adult plumage.

CHAP. V.

ASCENDING the steep cart road from the cove, and opening an old swing gate, immediately to the left we come to a road turning off at a right angle; this leads to the ruins of Porthkernou Chapel, a similar structure to those already noticed. Treryn or Pedn-vounder Cove is the next place to be visited. Pedn-vounder is the "headland with a road," which road is nothing more than a craggy path down the face of the cliff, which you descend as you would a ladder, placing the feet cautiously and grasping the patches of turf to prevent yourself from falling to the beach. It is impossible for a pathway to be nearer the perpendicular. But the smooth surface of the sandy beach beneath, and the appearance of Castle Treryn rising imposingly from the cove, have such a tempting influence, that one is induced to descend, even at the risk of breaking one's neck. When at the base of

CASTLE TRERYN.

the cliff the tourist will be more delighted than ever. The caverns, splendidly arched and open to the beach, are floored with beautiful shell sand: on entering them and looking seaward they have a most romantic aspect, and one almost expects to meet at the next turn some of the nereids, such as Frost has painted. No finer view of Castle Treryn can be had than this. The accompanying illustration is taken from near this spot; the Logan Rock is seen on the second ridge of rock inwards from the point.

The summit of the cliff must again be reached, to continue our course to the Logan Rock, still half a mile distant.

Many persons pass heedlessly over the mounds which stand on the land side of the isthmus connecting the promontory of Castle Treryn. By tracing what remains of these mounds they will be found to be of a regular form; for the original fortification consisted of three circular embankments one within the other; and every one who visits the Logan Rock passes an opening in another line of defence, running directly across the isthmus, as shown in the view on the next page.

This is a good example of the cliff castles, which in this manner intersect all the most important headlands along the coast. Who constructed them is unknown. Dr. Borlase says they are the works of the Danes, who, being invited to land by the Cornish to help them against the Saxons, intrenched and fortified their landing-places, and though in alliance with the natives, had many castles in the west of

Cornwall, in which they wintered. After Athelstan's conquest they turned enemies to their allies, and injured them as much as possible; these castles were then their strongholds. Polwhele endeavoured to

ENTRANCE TO CASTLE TRERYN.

prove that the Irish constructed them. And it has been argued that they could not be the works of the Cornish Britons, because they would never suffer themselves to be besieged in these headlands, where they could get neither food nor assistance; but if foreign enemies were to land and fortify the spot, they might always have access to their ships for provisions or for refuge.

Certainly such a chance would not be relied on, for it is only in the calmest weather that a boat can approach these rocks, and an interval of many weeks might elapse before this could be effected. And how is it possible that a number of men could descend from these perpendicular cliffs to the sea? The same objections would apply to the idea of their having been places of security for hoarding tin, which foreign freebooters are said to have taken from the mines, and guarded here until a favourable opportunity occurred to ship it. It has also been conjectured that these are Roman remains, and a Roman coin is said to have been found near Treryn. But this no more proves them Roman structures, than the finding of an English shilling on the plains of Waterloo would prove that any fortifications in Flanders were the works of the English. That the Romans did come into Cornwall is almost certain, but there is no evidence of their having raised fortifications. These cliff castles are, therefore, involved in mystery, which perhaps will never be cleared away, though it seems most probable they are British. Very little labour was required to fortify such headlands, for a handful of men might hold some of the passes against an army. Certain it is that this castle was not useless, for is not the very promontory called Treryn Dinas, " the castle of the fighting-place." These walls of rock then resounded with the cries of contending foes, with the twang of bows and the rattling of arms.

The rocks at the entrance to the promontory, and

rising above the line of defence, are remarkably fine, even for this grand coast, and show the cubical masses to great advantage. A rugged opening conducts to another pile, on which is the Logan Rock. This stone, which attracts a large number of visitors, is between sixty and seventy tons weight, and so nicely poised that a person can easily set it in a rocking or "logging" motion. There is no doubt of its being a natural curiosity, and several others, though none so large as this, may be seen in the district. Dr. Borlase said that it was "morally impossible that any lever, or, indeed, force (however applied in a mechanical way) could remove it." This statement, however, did not stand the test that Lieutenant Goldsmith, nephew to the poet, applied. In 1824, he had command of a cutter in the neighbourhood, and with ten or twelve of his men threw the rock from its balance, and it would have rolled into the sea, had it not been caught in the mouth of a chasm in the rocks in its descent. This exploit was not at all appreciated by the inhabitants of the neighbourhood; a great complaint was made about it, and the Lieutenant, at much expense, restored it to its original position. In aid of this object Davies Gilbert, the county historian, gave 25l., and applied to the Admiralty for the use of some machinery at Plymouth, which was granted. For a long time afterwards, the rock was kept chained and padlocked; as this, however, was considered absurd, the bonds were removed, and the rock is now at liberty; but it does not " log " so well as it did previous to its overthrow.

The Cornish antiquary considered this a rock deity

THE LOGAN ROCK.

of the Druids, and to have been used by them to impose on the people, as possessing the peculiar virtue of testing the guilt or innocence of persons accused of crime.

> "It moves obsequious to the gentlest touch
> Of him whose breast is pure ; but to a traitor,
> Tho' ev'n a giant's prowess nerv'd his arm,
> It stands as fixt as Snowdon."

The rock-basons, rounded hollows on the surface of granite rocks, on the same pile, are also pointed at as showing that the Druids had some connection with the spot. Dr. Borlase imagined that the rain and snow water caught in these vessels was used for lustration and purification; and that by the quantity, colour, motion, and other appearances, the priests judged of future events and dubious cases. These basons may be seen on almost all the high granite cairns in Cornwall. Dr. Borlase inclined to the opinion that some of them were artificial, but Dr. Paris, an eminent geologist, says " they are unquestionably the results of the operation of time and the elements, and have never been formed by any agents except those which nature employs in the decomposition of granitic masses. Their true nature is very easily traced by inspecting the rocks themselves. On examining the excavations they will always be found to contain distinct grains of quartz, and fragments of the other constituent parts of granite ; a small force is sufficient to detach from the sides of these cavities additional fragments, showing beyond doubt that a process of decomposition is still going on under favourable circumstances; these circumstances are the presence of water, or rather the action of air and moisture. If a drop of water can only make an effectual lodgment on a surface of this granite, a small cavity must sooner or later be produced; this insensibly enlarges as it becomes capable of holding more water, and the sides, as they continue to waste, necessarily retain an even and rounded cavity, on account of the uniform texture of the granite."

Whether they are natural or artificial, matters little as regards the use the Druids made of them, though it appears they generally used rocks in their natural state, the use of tools to work them into shape being forbidden.* Thus Dr. Paris's arguments, that they

---

* In evidence that the Druidism of this country resembled the idolatrous rites of the East, it is worthy of mention that rock-basons are yet found in India. "Both before and behind an enclosure, which contains the principal temples facing opposite ways, as well as in front of a smaller place of worship, about a furlong south-east of them, are large granite rocks, affording tolerably level surfaces of several feet square, respectively about four feet, two feet and a half, and a foot above ground. Each of these rocks exhibits a group of five basons; they are generally about six or eight inches in diameter, and perhaps a foot in depth, their brims are tolerably sharply cut, their sides are perfectly smooth, no trace of disintegration appears in either of them, and they are evidently of artificial origin. No symmetrical arrangement appears to prevail in their positions, and they are at irregular distances apart. The priests of the temples, as well as my native attendants, professed entire ignorance of any object for which these rock-basons were used; and on the subject of their religious rites generally, I found none of them communicative." *On the Rock Basons at Deo Dhoora, in Upper India.* By W. J. Henwood, Esq. F.R.S., F.G.S. &c. *Reports of the Royal Cornwall Institution,* 1857.

were not Druidic because natural, tend rather to defeat himself. Each visitor, however, will probably have his own opinion on the subject. One of these basons is called the " Giant's Chair."

The height of the pile on which the Logan Stone rests is thirty feet; this I measured by dropping a line from its summit. Towards the sea the rocks rise to a much greater height; the loftiest crag is Castle Peak, towering far above the others. Climb to its summit, look down its precipitous side to the sheets of foam around its base; on either hand are other noble masses, jutting up in towers and turrets and singular forms, most striking objects of wild magnificence.

The great and little Goular, " coral," Rocks are visible, and the coves of Porthkernou and Treryn have a pretty appearance from here. Around their sandy shores the sea is of a beautiful, transparent emerald; this colour is formed by the pale yellow of the sand seen through the delicate blue of the water. Sunset on a summer's evening, has a softening and glorious effect on this scene. The summits of the hills and rocks are touched with gold; the cliffs and declivities bathed in a purplish grey shade, blend seemingly into the ocean, or are faintly separated by a fine line of foam. On the tops of the rounded and rough acclivities, a few goats or sheep may be seen in the sunlight, their shadows streaming away to an indefinite length, until lost in the general gloom. A few birds wing their way across the brilliant clouds, the sea whispers in gentle sounds, and the little

groups of visitors, who were just now finding their
way over the rocks, have disappeared, and are on
their journey homeward.

> " Slow sank the sun into the sapphire sea,
>   Tinging the dimpling waters with his last
>   And loveliest beams of light, as the soft breeze
>   Of evening kiss'd the sea-nymphs, and the wave
>   Rose gently, and as gently fell again,
>   Soft murmuring. I stood beside a rock,
>   Whose rugged head look'd up into the sky.
>   Grey as the handle of the scythe of Time :
>   But lower down, between the martins' nests,
>   Rich ruby lichens in the sunset gleam'd
>   Like golden fingers clasping them around
>   Lest the rude winds should tear them ; and beneath,
>   A dark cliff beetled coldly o'er the deep,
>   Fringed by the lace-work of pearl-threaded foam
>   That mermaids weave and hang along the shore." *

No more fitting time than this to enjoy the repose
and the solitude, and to behold the magnificence of
these towering cliffs.

We have now seen the principal portion of the
granite coast of Bolerium ; my sketches and notes
will give the reader but a faint idea of the reality,
neither will the tourist by one excursion become
acquainted with the varied and ever-changing aspects
which these bold and romantic cliffs assume.   One
or two facts, however, will be observed, — that they
are almost all very precipitous, that there is no beach
except at three or four little sandy coves—and these

* Francis Hingeston, M.A., in *Colburn's New Monthly*, May,
1859.

are the only spots in which the waves roll in freely; elsewhere the rocks go down abruptly into the sea, and the waves are thrown back, broken to pieces, and put to confusion. Wild and mysterious is the scene when the clouds of mist from the south-west envelope the headlands like garments; sometimes the summits are entirely hidden, then clearing away, a shadowy belt is formed half way up the height, then descending to the turbulent surface of the sea, the white foam of the breakers is obscured, — but the muffled sound is heard, rising from "the cold grey stones," and resounding through the hollow caverns. Still the mist rolls on, breaking into masses, and rejoining its ragged edges over yawning chasms and "gulfs profound," getting denser as it goes, until the rising of the wind sends it away, or the sun in its strength pierces the gloom and sparkles on the crystals which the clouds have hung on the mosses and lichens of the rocks.

To be appreciated, the Land's End cliffs must be seen in calm and in storm, in sunshine and in cloud. Walk on the turf fragrant with wild flowers, sit amongst the sea pinks, and follow with the eye the numerous birds pursuing their vocations; watch the waves as they

> "play
> The summer hours away, — "

and the vessels as they creep along near the land — for the sky is fair and the sun is bright. How fearful is the change when the blasts howl and shriek around the cairns, and the deafening roar of the billows fills the air. The ships are far from land to avoid the iron-bound coast; it is destruction to near these cliffs. The huge waves raise their angry crests

> " on high,
> Into the tempest-cloud that blurs the sky,
> Holding rough dalliance with the fitful blast,
>   Whose stiff breath, whistling shrill,
>   Pierces with deadly chill
> The wet crew, feebly clinging to their shattered mast."

Thus the natural appearance of the coast is changed by the influence of the atmosphere, presenting in turn splendid effects for the study of the artist. The cumulus clouds which sometimes hang over the sea are of the grandest character, whilst the glory of the sunsets, especially when seen from the Land's End, are only equalled by those witnessed on the southern coasts of Europe.

We cannot take leave of the Logan Rock, and the parish of St. Levan with its romantic scenery, without noticing, and adding to the illustrations of the natural history of the district, another species of British bird, lately found in this locality. It is a female specimen of the roller, a bird about the size of a jay, and ap pears to belong to the pie tribe. The assemblage of the most beautiful tints of blue, from ultramarine to the richest violet, gives this bird a claim to vie with the parrots in brilliancy of plumage; but its chief value as a British bird is its extreme rarity.

And if it happens to be spring time, the green turf about the Treryn cliffs will be seen overspread here and there with masses of blue, produced by the beautiful flowers of the *Scilla verna.* At St. Ives it varies with white and pink flowers.

THE ROLLER.

The village of Treryn, pronounced Treen, is somewhat more than half a mile from the Logan Rock; an inn there affords accommodation "for man and beast." Thence the road descends very abruptly into the valley which terminates at Penberth; it is known by the name of "Burian Bottoms." Some parts of it are richly clothed in foliage, and picturesque cottages are found beside the little trout stream. The road on the opposite side is equally steep, but more continuous. Nothing of importance will be observed by the wayside for the next two or three miles, when we arrive at St. Burian.

From its historical associations this is one of the most interesting spots in Cornwall. It was first rendered sacred by the residence of " St. Buriana, a holy woman of Ireland," who was held in high veneration as a " goodly saint," and did much to reclaim the natives from their idolatrous practices. When she had ceased from her toils they laid her body near her hermitage, which then became an oratory. So great was her fame that Athelstan, after his victory at Bolleit, knelt at her shrine, praying for the success of his intended enterprise to the Isles of Scilly, making a vow that, if God blest him, he would raise on this ground a collegiate church. Returning from his conquest he forgot not his promise, and, about the year 930, founded and endowed the church, dedicating it to St. Buriana. " He gave lands and tithe of a considerable value for ever, himself becoming the first patron thereof, as his successors, the Kings of England, have been ever since." Augustine canons and three prebendaries presided over the establishment. The accompanying cut will give an idea of the appearance of the class of venerable monks who once made this place a seat of learning. " The canons secular of St. Augustine were the clergy of the cathedral and collegiate churches, who lived in a community on the monastic model. Their habit was a long black cassock (the parochial clergy did not then universally wear black), over which, during divine service, they wore a surplice and a fur tippet,

called an *almuce*, and a square black cap, called
a *baret*, and at other times a black cloak and hood
with a leather girdle; according to their rule they
might wear their beards, but, from the thirteenth
century downwards, we find them usually shaven." *

AUGUSTINIAN CANON.

Athelstan also granted to the church the privilege
of "sanctuary." The remains of an ancient building,
south of the present church, were to be seen till within
the last few years, called "the Sanctuary;" the spot
still retains the name, and an ancient cross may be
seen near it.

Subsequently, a dean was appointed, by one of

* Engraving and note from the Art-Journal, 1856.

ROOD SCREEN, ST. BURIAN.

the popes, over the canons and prebends. The
deanery consisted, as it does to this day, of the
parishes of St. Burian, St. Levan, and St. Sennen,
and was held from the king by the service of saying
a hundred masses and a hundred psalters for the
souls of the king and his ancestors. It was, however,
seized entirely into the king's hands in the time of
Edward III., under the pretence that John de
Mount, the third dean, was a Frenchman. In
proof of a Frenchman having some connection with
this locality, a curious seal, probably of the four-
teenth century, was found here some time since,
bearing the inscription, "*Sigillum Confraternitatis
Conceptionis Beatœ Mariœ Ordinis Sancti Augus-
tini Parisiis.*" *

What remained of Athelstan's college was destroyed during Cromwell's usurpation by the notorious
Shrubsall. No remains, therefore, of the large establishment that the Saxon King founded here now
exist. This is not to be wondered at, as most
probably, the greater part of the buildings were of
wood. The present church of St. Burian, however,
is one of the finest in Cornwall. It possessed a
magnificent rood screen and loft, of the fifteenth
century, and consists of a nave and two aisles; the
tower is one of the loftiest in the county, and
standing on high ground, 519 feet above the sea,
is the most conspicuous structure in the whole
district.

* An engraving of this seal is given in "The ancient Crosses and
other Antiquities of Cornwall."

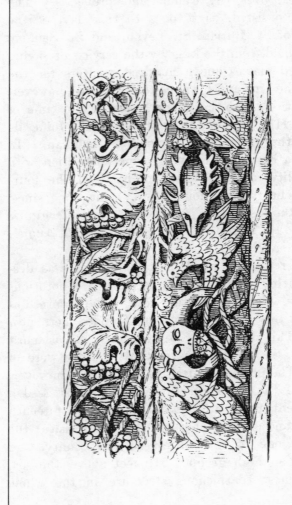

ROOD SCREEN, ST. BURIAN.

ROOD SCREEN, ST. BURIAN.

In the projection, shown in the cut, between the
two middle windows of the south side, is a spiral
stairway of stone, conducting to the rood-loft, of
which some fragments may yet be seen. A portion
like a huge beam extends from the top of this stairway, across the south aisle and the nave; it is
elaborately carved on both sides, and was richly
gilt and painted, chiefly with red and blue, but now
much faded. The upper part is bordered, the
entire length, with a vine pattern; bunches of grapes,
appearing betwixt the leaves, are, in some instances,
pecked at by birds, or grasped by unseemly demons.
On the lower part, across the nave, the representations
are of a fragmentary character, consisting of heads
of various animals peeping through openings in the
foliage; some have horns, some resemble monkeys,
others grin and twist their countenances into the

ROOD SCREEN, ST. BURIAN.

most horrible contortions; on the side facing the
altar, a creature like a cat seizes two birds, one in

each claw; on the western side, a bird descends on a long-eared head, a serpent creeps away from beneath it. On the line of carving which crosses the aisle, complete scenes are represented: first comes a hunter, with a staff or cross-bow in his hand, exciting his dogs to the chase; one, which is connected to himself by a leash, has caught a bird; farther on others are springing on a deer. Then follows a strange piece of work, a demon, painted bluish-black, grasps in one hand the end of a scroll, biting it savagely with his grinning teeth; with the other hand he holds a bird by the wing, a deer seizes this bird by the other wing; on the left a bird pinches the ear of the demon. At the southern extremity is curiously depicted a patient animal of some kind, which a red dragon has seized by the throat, whilst a bird attacks him from behind.

Throughout the work it will be observed that the creatures are at variance with each other; birds are sometimes allied with the demons in their deeds of cruelty, in other cases they are themselves preyed on. In one instance, something like a coat of arms is shown, — a shield bearing a two-headed eagle and a fish, over the eagle is a fleur-de-lis.

The breadth of this piece of work is about eighteen inches, or from that to two feet. A gilded twist, resembling the cable moulding, runs along the top and bottom, a similar line separates the vine from the lower part. The workmanship is very rude, yet it has a bold effect — every detail being distinctly seen from the floor. The lower portion of the rood-screen consists of panels, the carvings generally being scroll patterns; the connecting framework is wanting. Some fragments of this elaborate structure are preserved in boxes in the church. It is deeply to be regretted that splendid church decorations are so often at the mercy of the ignorant. About fifty years ago much of the screen was perfect; but from some fancied notion that it deadened the preacher's voice, it was barbarously pulled down. Some portions were used for the vilest purposes, and profanely converted into doors for pigs' styes.

A clergyman* who recently had charge of the living, collected together as much as he could recover of the missing work, and caused the upper portion, which I have noticed and partially illustrated, to be placed in its original position.

Although these designs might appear very whimsical to many, there can be no doubt that they contain some hidden meaning, and were intended either to rebuke the thoughtless, or to present some sacred symbol to the pious. On the fragments engraved in this volume, I have received the following remarks from the Rev. R. S. Hawker, of Morwenstow.

"'*Ubi aves ibi angeli.*' Wheresoever there are birds there are spirits, is an axiom of faith. They were born from water. They inhabit air. They are classed as clean and unclean, evil and good. In the Old Testament, the eagle symbolised the presence of

* The Rev. Edward Seymour.

the paraclete: after the time of Elijah, who pro-
mised a double portion of his spirit to Elisha, the
eagle sometimes had in symbol, two necks. In the
New Testament a dove announced the action of the
third person of the Trinity.

"Thus a bird came to be the signal of a spirit.
*Respicite volatilia cœli. Considerate corvos. Vene-
runt volucres. Venit Satanas.* These phrases suggested themes of thought.

"In antique carvure, birds usually denote good
spirits, and beasts of prey the demons. The warfare
between these for the souls of men is quaintly carved
in St. Burian screen.

"The vine is the church. The demons assail its
growth and clusters. Said the Rune,— *Capite nobis
vulpes parvulas quæ demoliuntur vineas.* Among
the Gentiles the augur prophesied events from the
demeanour of birds and the aspect of animals in
sacrifice.

"The deer attacked by the dragon, is an accustomed type of Christ, and also of a Christian man:
when assailed by wolves it simply typifies the on-
slaught of demons on the solitary soul.

"The fish is the well known type of a baptized
person." *

Within the screen are rude oak stalls, called
"misereres," with movable seats which may either
be lifted up or let down, such as the old chair and

---

* The fish was used by the early Christians as a secret symbol for
the name of Jesus Christ; the letters of the Greek word 'ΙΧΘΥΣ
stood as the initials for Jesus Christ, Son of God, Saviour.

seat discovered in St. German's church*; these, Whitaker considered the stalls of the dean and prebendaries;—the interior of the church he says "is still disposed nearly as Athelstan left it."

This writer believed this to be the veritable church of Athelstan, and accounts for the fresh appearance of the exterior of the building "from the frequent washings to which its high position on a hill, and its pointed exposure to the rains of the

ST. BURIAN CHURCH.

Atlantic, continually subject it." A wonderful instance this of the inaccuracy of even learned men, less than a century ago, in architectural subjects. Whitaker's architectural disquisitions upon St. Ger-

* See "Ancient Crosses, &c. in East Cornwall."

man's church, in his otherwise useful book, "The Ancient Cathedral of Cornwall," are as worthless as they are elaborate, and quite as absurd as his attributing to the age of Athelstan a tower and church erected in the fifteenth and sixteenth centuries.

On the floor, within the walls of the tower, is a long stone, coffin-shaped, with a Norman French inscription, in rude characters, around the border. In English it reads:—

" ✠ Clarice, the wife of Geoffry de Bolleit, lies here: God on her soul have mercy: who prays for her soul shall have ten days' pardon. Amen."

Another monument near this, standing against the wall, is thus inscribed:—

"Here lyes the body of Arthur Levelis of Trewoof in this parish, Esq., who departed this life the 2nd day of May, Anno Dom. 1671.

"This worthy family hath flourished here,
Since William's Conquest, full six hundred year;
And longer much it might But that the Blest
Must spend their Seauenths in a Blessed Rest;
But yet this Gentleman (Last of his Name)
Hath by his Virtues Eterniz'd the same
Much more than children could or Bookes, for Loue
Records it here in Heartes in Life Aboue."

The font, of Ludgvan granite, similar to others in the county, is ornamented by scroll work and crosses, and was supported by four shafts.

The stoup at the doorway is mutilated; a head appears to have been carved on the bason, but it is knocked off. The corbel over the doorway was perhaps intended to receive the figure of the Blessed

Virgin or the patron saint; this also is wanting. We must give the Roundheads credit for these mutilations.

ST. BURIAN CHURCHYARD.

Near the porch stands a pretty cross on a flight of steps; on one side of it is carved the figure of our Lord; on the reverse, are five bosses, symbolical of the five wounds in His body. It was the custom thus to place a cross near the southern entrance to the church, suggesting due preparation previously to entering the sacred building. Near this cross is a tombstone with the following curious epitaph : —

> " Our Life is but a Winter's Day ;
> Some only Breakfast and away ;
> Others to Dinner stay and are Full fed ;
> The oldest only Sups and goes to Bed ;
> Large is his Debt, who Lingers out the Day :
> Who goes the Soonest has the least to Pay."

Without the churchyard is another cross, broken and defaced, standing on a walled base. There is a tradition that the burial-ground once extended around this monument. Hals suggests that the spot might have been so used before the church was built, and says that the word Bury-an signifies a "burying-place." This, however, is a mere play on words.

Pendrea, the "principal town," about half a mile west of the church, was the property of William Noye, Attorney-General to Charles I., who died in 1635, and was buried in the church of St. Mawgan. The old house at Pendrea in which he was born has been recently taken down.

The road from St. Burian to Penzance passes over a fine open country, affording extensive views, but there is nothing of particular interest by the way-side, besides what has been already noticed.

THE BROWN LONGBEAKED SNIPE. (See p. 92.)

CHAP. VI.

THERE are twelve parishes west of St. Michael's
Mount; they are all partially bounded by the sea,—
except Sancreed. The church of this parish is
pleasantly situated and embowered in trees; but
possesses no architectural features of particular
interest. A carved fragment of the rood-screen, now
thrown aside as lumber, is, however, worthy of notice.
The cross in the churchyard is one of the finest in the
county; it is more than seven feet high, and bears
several curious devices, among others, the lily of the
Blessed Virgin.

The name of this parish has been much speculated
on, as there is no particular account of such a saint
as Sancreed. In the taxation of Pope Nicholas, A. D.
1291, it is called " *Ecclesia Sancti Mancredi;* " and
in another MS. " *Sancti Sancredi.*" M for S is an

obvious blunder of the original scribe. In the Valor
Ecclesiasticus, temp. Henry VIII., it is spelt
"Sancret." Davies Gilbert says the people pro-
nounce the word "San-crist," and suggests whether

SANCREED CHURCH.

the church is not really dedicated to the Saviour of
mankind, and the name equivalent, in fact, to Christ
Church. Some will have it to be "San-crus," the
"Holy Cross."

On the summit of a hill, a mile west of the church,
are the remains of Caer Bran, "Brennius's Castle."
It consisted of a stone wall about twelve feet thick;
two ditches and an earthen embankment; and a
circular building of stone, appears to have stood in
the centre. It is now little more than a heap of
ruins—though its circular form may be distinctly

traced. At the western base of the hill is an old road, óf which some portions are paved with flat stones. As the Romans made their principal ways near fortifications in a similar manner, it will probably be attributed to them, by those who fancy that the Romans had permanent establishments in Cornwall. Near Cairn Uny, close at hand, is a curious subterranean gallery, walled on the sides, and covered with flat slabs of granite; it is partly fallen in, and cannot easily be entered.

In this locality also, is the famous well of St. Uny; the spring still rises from the soil, as of yore, clear and sparkling; but the walls of the little baptistery have long since been demolished. Two or three of the arched stones of the doorway or window, may yet be seen on the spot.

The dark and dreary hill of Bartiné ascends from here; this was also crowned with a castle. Bar-tiné, is the "hill of fires," and was probably used as a signal station for communicating intelligence in time of danger; almost every parish in the county had its beacon for this purpose. Or, the word may refer to a practice of primitive times, when huge fires were kindled on the hill-tops by the sun-worshippers — "on the very moment of the solstice." "A feu-de-joie, kindled the very moment the year began : for the first of all years, or the most ancient that we know of, began at the month of June." The custom is still observed in the neighbourhood, at midsummer, on the eves of St. John the Baptist and St. Peter. Though these saints appear the osten-

sible object of veneration, the ceremony is of Pagan
origin, and was diverted to their honour by the early
Christians, who, whenever it was possible, used the
heathen monuments, and some of their practices, for
the purpose of bringing them to their own faith.
The lighting of fires on the hills seems somewhat to
have declined within the last few years; and the
ceremony is now chiefly kept up at Penzance, by
brilliant displays of fireworks; but little regard is
paid either to the sun or to the saints.

Cairn Brea is an adjoining hill, 689 feet high; on
its rocky summit stood a little chapel, supplanting,
probably, a Druidical temple or altar. It is supposed
to have been a chantry, for the celebration of religious
services for the safety of mariners. It was " a free,
privileged, manumised chapel," says Hals, " where
the bishop could not visit." Although the structure
has disappeared, it is worth while to climb the hill
for the sake of the extensive view. St. Michael's
Mount appears as if rising out of an inland lake, and
both the north and south channels are seen, — the
sea-line embracing twenty-nine points of the com-
pass. These hills are in the parish of St. Just.

The high road from Penzance to St. Just church
is of little interest to the tourist. This part of the
coast is chiefly visited on account of its extensive
and wonderful mining operations, which in their
progress have destroyed many valuable objects of
antiquity.

St. Just offers no great attractions to the botanist,
but the sportsman may find employment in some

localities. The little bustard*, rarely seen in this part of the world, has been procured from this parish.

THE LITTLE BUSTARD.

The church is a fine building, with a lofty granite tower. From the numerous fragments of carved stone, capitals, &c., found when some alterations were

---

* The illustrations of birds, in this volume, were made from specimens preserved by the well-known taxidermist, Mr. W. H. Vingoe, of Penzance. Mr. Vingoe has a valuable collection of the birds found in the district.

being made in the church, it is evident that this is not the first that has occupied the site. A monumental stone then discovered, has an inscription in Roman capitals,—" SILVS HIC IACET ; " on the reverse side is a cross. But who this Silus was is unknown ; it has been conjectured that he was one of the Irish missionaries who accompanied St. Patrick into this country in the fifth century, for the purpose of preaching the Gospel.

Some of the capitals in this church are elaborately sculptured, representing the arms of the Boscawens and other principal families connected with the parish, and other designs of a more sacred order. The bells have inscriptions : on the largest, the following has been deciphered — " St. Just bell, cast at St. Erth, 1741. So bless King George, James Reynolds, James Tregeare, and Admiral Vernon, churchwardens."

This was about the time of the admiral's victories in the West Indies, and it seems, that in token of respect, the parishioners named him as an honorary churchwarden for that year. The two other bells are older, and were cast in those days " when great attention was paid to holy things erected in the sanctuary ; when every bell was dedicated to a saint whose name it subsequently bore." Thus the second bell was called " St. Michael," and the third " St. Mary." One has the following inscription : —

" St. Michael, ora pro nobis."

On the other,—

> "Protege virgo pia,
> Quos convoco Sancta Maria." *

The church was dedicated to St. Justus, who was sent to England by Pope Gregory, A.D. 596, with St. Augustine and other monks, to convert the Saxons.

The name of the original church was Lafrouda, written in ancient deeds, Lafroudha and Lafroodha. The Rev. J. Buller gives the following explanation: Laf or Lan, the Cornish for a church, and Rhoodha, a corruption of the Saxon word rood, signifying a cross, or image of the crucifixion. Dha, in Cornish as in Welsh, is good; so Lafrouda may signify the "Church of the good Cross."

Of St. Just there is a popular tradition, certainly not very favourable to the character of that saint. He went to visit St. Keverne, who resided near the Lizard, and was most hospitably received. After enjoying each other's company for some hours, St. Just remarked that as he had some distance to go it was time to start, so taking an affectionate leave, he grasped his staff, and strode away on his journey homeward; he had not been long gone, however, before St. Keverne found that some of his most valuable relics were missing. There was no mistaking who took them, so picking up some loose rocks on Crouza Down, about a quarter of a ton

---

* A more elaborate description of this church, with engravings of some of its architectural details, will be found in the Rev. J. Buller's "Account of the Parish of St. Just."

weight each, he started in pursuit. As St. Just had expected this, he had made the best use of his time, and had arrived at Germoe before his angry and injured brother overtook him. On the property being demanded, he sturdily refused to make restitution. Whereupon St. Keverne had recourse to his ammunition, which he used to such advantage, that St. Just was compelled to drop the plunder and fly. In evidence of the veracity of the story of this combat, the stones that were dropped are still seen by the road side, between Penzance and Helston. They are composed of what is commonly called iron-stone, none of which is to be found elsewhere in the neighbourhood ; but it is plentifully scattered over Crouza Down, the course taken by the fugitive and his pursuer.

There can be no doubt that this legend is founded entirely on the appearance of the rocks ; the people having had no other means of accounting for their presence on that spot. It is but another expression of the popular belief in giants, though it seems unfair that the good fame of St. Just should be sullied merely for the sake of giving shape to the story.

St. Just is a large, populous village, chiefly inhabited by persons engaged in mining. It possesses a neat building for the accommodation of the members of the " Literary Institution." Library, reading-room, and lecture-hall, are well arranged, and would do credit to any of the towns in the county.

An object of interest here is the old amphitheatre, or rather the remains of one, in which plays were

enacted. These were written and spoken in the
Cornish language, and "were composed for begetting
in the people a right notion of the Scriptures." As
the sacred persons of the Trinity were represented,
much profanity must have prevailed in such spectacles.
This circle was a hundred and twenty-six feet in diameter ; the seats, which ran around the sides, consisted
of six steps, each about one foot high. There were
other similar structures in the county, and they were
called " Plânanguares,"—" places of sport or amusement."

CAPE CORNWALL.

Cape Cornwall, a mile and a half from the village,
is one of the most prominent headlands of the western
coast. It differs in character from those already
noticed, on account of the slate formation, which

extends to Pendeen, commencing here. Its upper part is a huge, rounded hillock, forming a slippery declivity on either side. On the summit was a beacon or watch-tower. Dr. Borlase speaks of Cape Cornwall "as the promontorie of Helenus, so called, as some think, because Helenus, the son of Priamus, who arrived here with Brute, lieth buried here, except the sea have washed away his sepulchre."

On the isthmus, the remains of an ancient chapel within its original enclosure, may still be seen; it is called Parc-an-chapel, the "chapel field." The building, with some modern additions, is now used as a cattle-shed: it was known as St. Helen's Oratory. In a watercourse near the ruins a small stone cross

GABLE-CROSS OF ST. HELEN'S ORATORY.

was found, supposed to have been the gable-cross attached to this structure. It bears a monogram, the two initial letters of the Greek word Christ, which was frequently used by the early Christians, as well as in mediæval times.

A line of defence severed this promontory from the mainland. The building on the edge of the

cliff, which is seen in the cut, is an old deserted
engine-house, used for the mine which was worked
there. The sketch is taken from Priest's Cove,
which has a sandy beach, on which a few fishing
boats are kept, chiefly the property of miners, ·who
in the summer months find time for fishing.

Nearly a mile south-west of the cape are the
Brisons, two fearful and dangerous rocks, rising
about sixty or seventy feet above high-water mark;
they are sometimes called the Sisters. Brison is
Cornish for prison; and tradition says, that as

THE BRISONS.

prisons they were anciently used. A wreck, one of
the most melancholy which has happened on the
coast, occurred here about eleven years ago. During
a thick fog and strong gale, early on a Saturday
morning, a brig, bound from Liverpool to the Spanish

Main, struck between these rocks, and of course immediately went to pieces. The crew, nine men, with one woman, the wife of the master, got on the ledge. They were discovered from the shore as soon as day broke, but it was then impossible to render them any assistance. In this wretched condition they remained until about nine o'clock, when a tremendous wave rose, and carried them all off. Seven out of the ten at once sank. Of the remaining three, one, a mulatto, contrived to get on a portion of floating wreck, and after being buffeted about for some hours, he managed, with remarkable coolness and presence of mind, by means of a plank, which he used as a paddle, and a piece of canvas, which served him for a sail, with the assistance of the strong tides, to keep clear of the boiling surf. Whilst this poor fellow was thus struggling for life, being anxiously watched by a crowd of persons on shore, five fishermen belonging to Sennen, determined, with their usual resolute and fearless spirit, to launch their boat through the breakers; in this they succeeded, and after encountering great risk, rescued the mulatto.

When the master and his wife were carried off the ledge, they were washed to the Little Brison. The master first got a footing, and then assisted his wife, and for a time, both were in comparative safety. Whilst the fishermen were engaged in saving the mulatto, the revenue cutter from Penzance was seen working round the Land's End, being ordered to the spot by the commander. A boat put off from her, but was soon compelled to return. The gale still continuing, nothing more could be done for the day; so the cutter hove to, and the captain hoisted colours to encourage the poor sufferers, and to let them know that they were not deserted. They were now to spend the night on the desolate rock, without food or shelter, exposed to all the fury of the wind and rain. On Sunday morning the wind abated a little, and several boats put off, but none could approach within 100 yards of the rock. At last a boat was seen making towards the spot, manned by the coastguard. The commander, Captain Davies, now, at great personal risk, proceeded to throw a line by help of a rocket; the first which was fired carried the line to the rock, but it again fell into the sea; the second happily fell close to the man, who seized it and fastened it around the waist of his wife, who after much persuasion gave the fearful leap. But when drawn to the boat, life was almost extinct, aud she died before she could be got on shore; the captain then tied the cord around himself, and was dragged greatly exhausted to the boat.

When a wreck occurs on the coast, the noble and fearless conduct of the Cornishmen cannot be exceeded. At such times, as, indeed, in all times of danger, they show the most heroic courage, and risk their own lives to save the shipwrecked mariner. From the numerous brave deeds performed on such occasions, the Cornish have become justly celebrated; and though the iron-bound coast may present a frowning and forbidding aspect to the storm-driven sailor, there are on these rocky cliffs generous hearts ready to receive, and strong arms stretched forth to save.

Caraglose, or more properly Caregluz, the "grey rock," rises at the southern extremity of Priest's Cove ; it is, in some respects, the finest headland of this parish. At this spot is a high, narrow cavern, and one of the most interesting raised beaches in the district.

Hence to Sennen Cove there are some points of great interest, although the tract is exposed and has a desolate appearance. Even from the names only of the rocks and headlands some idea may be formed of its character. At Bosorn and Bollowal cliffs, or rather on the side of the hill overhanging the sea, are old mine workings, whence it is supposed the Phœnicians were supplied with tin. These old works consist of chasms opened along the surface of the ground ; in this manner, with much unnecessary labour, the ancients sought for tin. The miners call these places " coffins." The ancients cast their metal into form on the spot; and some pieces of tin, smelted into rude shapes, have been discovered in some parts of this parish. In support of the belief that the Phœnicians traded and had intercourse with this locality, a bronze figure of a bull, a sacred emblem among that people, is shown. It was found near the vicarage, and has every appearance of great antiquity : some of the most learned antiquaries pronounced it to be Phœnician. Here then may the tourist rest awhile by the stern and rugged cliffs, and picture to himself the scenes when the prows of eastern galleys ploughed these turbulent seas.

Proceeding southward, the next cove is Porthnanven, "port of the high valley;" there is a remarkable raised beach here, a continuation of that mentioned at Caregluz. The other points in succession are:—Cairn Hermên, "the long-stone cairn;" Cairn y Withan, "the oak-tree cairn;" there is a large iron vein, six feet wide, in the cliff here. At Proge Cove, is a natural arch, accessible at low water, from Porthnanven. Cairn Leskys, the " cairn of light;" Cairn Greeb, or Gribba, "rocks like a bird's crest or comb;" the Radjill Cliff; Maen Dower, "the stone near the water;" Pol Pry, "clay pool," Cove, two caverns here whose roofs are formed with boulders; Cairn Creis, the "middle cairn," its summit was crowned with a beacon; Cairn Ding Dong; Cairn Clougy, "the cairn of hard rock." At Nanjulian, "the valley of hazels," the coast becomes much lower; a stream runs down here, and immediately south of it, there is another fine raised beach, consisting of boulders and pebbles : it is seen for a length of about a hundred and fifty feet, and is about six feet thick; the lower part is from fifteen to sixteen feet above the sea at high water. Mellyn, "yellow," Cairn; Gazick Cove; Cairn Creagle, "the crying cairn;" it is also called the "watch cairn;" probably signals were given on this height by shouting. Cairn Venton Lês or Lêswell, the "cairn near the well," the well is close at hand; Cairn Aire, "the inner point," or "cairn of slaughter;" Gwynver, "green sand" Cove. Then comes a rivulet which separates the parishes of St. Just and St. Sennen; beyond this is Cairn Hoar, the "sister's cairn." The greater number of these names were given from the natural appearance of the spots; others are derived from some connecting history or legend, which would be interesting to know.

Along this tract the *Samolus Valerandi*, water pimpernel, is frequently met with; it bears small

SAMOLUS VALERANDI.

whitish flowers, and was highly regarded by the ancients. The Druids gathered it in a ritual religious manner; he that was to perform the office, was to do it fasting; to use the left hand only, and whilst engaged in this duty, he was not to look behind him on any account, nor to lay down the herbs anywhere but in the cistern where the cattle drank, from which it kept off disease.

Lotus angustissimus and *Teucrium Chamœdrys* may also be found in St. Just.

In his wanderings along the coast, the tourist will observe many beautiful and interesting plants which are not noticed in these pages. For the phænogamous plants and ferns of the western part of Cornwall, the reader is referred to a list in the reports of the Natural History and Antiquarian Society of Penzance, by Dr. J. B. Montgomery, who possesses' beautifully preserved specimens of all of them, and to whom I have to express my thanks for access to this valuable collection, in some instances when the plants I required were out of season.

From Cape Cornwall, Kenidjack headland is seen to the north ; this was also fortified, and some remains of the walls and ditch may yet be seen. Porthleden is the name of the cove between these promontories. Skirting the coast from Castle Kenidjack, many fine " bits " of rocky scenery will be passed.

At the Bunny cliffs, a little south of Botallack, ancient tin workings, supposed to be Phœnician, will again be observed ; they are open to the surface, and have a strange and curious appearance.

Perhaps no headland along this coast has such a savage and fearful aspect as Botallack. The engine-houses perched on its rocky crags, contrast with the wild magnificence of nature, and render the scene still more impressive. Down these perpendicular

BOTALLACK MINE.

walls of rock, heavy machinery and building materials had to be lowered 200 feet, for the construction
of an engine-house; half-way up the height is
another; the third is on the summit.

This mine is worked one third of a mile under the
bed of the sea, the rolling of the boulders to and fro,
and the roaring of the waves overhead, are distinctly
heard by the miners when at work.*   Visitors often
descend to the "crown engine," which is so-called
from being situated near the rocks named "the Three
Crowns."

Many valuable specimens of minerals have been
found here; such as, arseniate of iron; sulphuret of
bismuth; native copper; specular iron ore; hydrous
oxide of iron, &c. The geological features of the
spot are also of great interest.

The botanist may discover in this locality, *Inula
crithmoides*, and *Hypericum linariifolium.*

* The effect produced by the roaring of the waves overhead has
been thus described by Mr. W. J. Henwood : —

"I was once, however, underground in Wheal Cock (a mine adjoining Botallack), during a storm. At the extremity of the level,
seaward, some eighty or one hundred fathoms from the shore, little
could be heard of its effects, except at intervals, when the reflux of
some unusually large wave projected a pebble outward bounding and
rolling over the rocky bottom. But when standing beneath the
base of the cliff, and in that part of the mine, where but nine feet of
rock stood between us and the ocean, the heavy roll of the large
boulders, the ceaseless grinding of the pebbles, the fierce thundering
of the billows, with the crackling and boiling as they rebounded,
placed a tempest in its most appalling form too vividly before me, to
be ever forgotten. More than once doubting the protection of our
rocky shield, we retreated in affright, and it was only after repeated
trials that we had confidence to pursue our investigation."

Dr. Borlase describes some Druidical circles, intersecting each other in a curious manner, which existed on the Botallack, "high dwelling," estate; not a vestige of them is now to be seen.

The Levant, another submarine mine, about a mile distant, is as worthy of a visit as Botallack.

Continuing our course northward, the next point of interest is Pendeen, or Pendinas, the "castled headland." A little way out at sea are some rocks called the Wra or Three-Stone Oar. The shore of Pendeen Cove is composed of fine sand; a few fishing boats are kept here; and it is also a coast-guard station.

The granite recommences at this place, intersecting the slate in narrow and peculiar veins. Cairn Kenidzhek, is the "hooting cairn;" Cairn Ros, the "cairn of heath or moss."

Pendeen House, nearly half a mile up from the coast, is a good example of the style of country gentlemen's houses two hundred years ago; it bears the date of 1670, but portions are probably older. It is to be chiefly noticed, however, as the house in which the celebrated Cornish historian and antiquary, Dr. William Borlase, was born, in the year 1695. "Having received," says Davies Gilbert, "a proper introductory education, he was sent to Exeter College, Oxford, once (and to a great extent still) the college generally resorted to by the gentlemen from the west, where he took the degree of M. A. in 1719. In 1720 he entered into holy orders, and in 1722 obtained the rectory of Ludgvan, in Cornwall, which

was followed in 1732 by the vicarage of St. Just,
The former place was his residence for the last fifty-
two years of his life; here he pursued his studies with
persevering ardour, and gratified the admirers of

PENDEEN.

literature by arranging and publishing, in 1754,
'Antiquities of Cornwall;' in 1756, a work on the
antiquities of the Scilly Islands, and in 1758 the
'Natural History of Cornwall.' In consequence of
an essay on Cornish crystals, he was elected a fellow
of the Royal Society in 1750; he also received the
degree of LL.D. from the University of Oxford." He
corresponded with Pope, and presented him with some
valuable ores and metals; on one occasion he sent
him a Cornish diamond, which the poet thus acknow-
ledges: "I have received your gift, and have so placed

it in my grotto, that it will resemble the donor, in the shade, but shining. "

Dr. Borlase has been censured by some writers for surcharging his works with too many ebullitions of imagination; it is also said that the advancement of science has proved much of his writing erroneous. But as Davies Gilbert justly remarks, " he rather merits praise than condemnation for his ebullitions of imagination and conjectures, since these may have led others to strictly examine them, and elicit useful discoveries from his involuntary errors."

Dr. Borlase's " Antiquities," has become a text-book for all who write on the ancient remains of the county; those who have affected to despise it most have quoted it oftenest; his conclusions are sometimes presented to the public as startling and fanciful; but his arguments should be read from his own works, then will it be seen that modern writers, with all the aid of the " advancement of science," have little or no advantage over him. His works display a depth of research, a patient industry and ability which few writers of the present day bring to bear on subjects of a similar character.

Within a few yards of the house is an ancient cave or " Vau," which might have been a subject of speculation to the doctor from his earliest years. It consists of three passages; the first runs in a straight line, and is twenty-eight feet in length, at its extremity two others branch off, one on either side. The sides are walled up, and incline towards each other on the top, the better to receive the flat

slabs with which it is covered. This cave is similar
to that at Bolleit and others in the district. It is
uncertain to what use they were appropriated, although they are generally supposed to have been places
of security for the ancient British. The Pendeen Vau
is now partially fallen in; the outer passage may be
followed to its extremity, but there the fallen stones
obstruct the farther progress of the explorer. It was
for a long time regarded superstitiously by the
people of the neighbourhood, and was supposed by
them to communicate with the sea, half a mile
distant, and to be the haunt of some terrible spirit.

I had some conversation with a miner lately,
respecting this cave. He told me that a comrade
of his once determined to explore it, and that he
went a considerable way under the sea, indeed so far
that he got afraid: he burnt a pound of candles during
the time he was travelling. He said, here and there
by the sides of the passage, there were little recesses
with a bench or seat in each, " these, you know," says
the miner, " were put to ' touch your pipe a bit;' "
a Cornish phrase for resting awhile. And he had no
doubt, that if his friend had continued his journey,
he would have arrived dryshod at the Scilly Islands,
about twenty-six miles distant !

The northern part of St. Just is a dreary wild, yet
interesting even for its dreariness. The church of
Pendeen occupies as barren and bleak a site as could
be chosen from one end of the land to the other. It
is a fine building, designed by the first clergyman of
the district, the Rev. Robert Aitken, on the plan of

the ancient cathedral of Iona, and built, almost
entirely by the people for themselves. It harmonises
well with the romantic spot in which it has been reared,
a spot scarcely less bleak and wintry than Iona itself.

Cairn Kenidzhek*, commonly, but erroneously,
spelt Kenidjack, stands near the northern roadway
to Penzance; being 640 feet above the sea, it is a

CAIRN KENIDZHEK.

very conspicuous object for several miles round; the
rocks on the summit assume the most fantastic
forms, and an arrangement irregular and strange. The
surrounding country exhibits one monotonous tint of
blackish brown, broken here and there by a few grey
rocks appearing above the surface; stunted heath
endeavours to thrive on this sterile soil, but the
piercing blasts which sweep over this unsheltered

* "The hooting cairn, so called probably from the significant
prophetic noises which consecrated rocks were supposed by the
ancients sometimes to emit."

tract, check all vegetation. Macbeth's witches might
have danced on such a spot. Yet is there an attraction about this hoary cairn which must render it of
interest to all. Its solitary and desolate aspect is
one feature; a deep silence and mysteriousness hang
over it, — the spirit of the past seems to reign here,
for the spot is now as it ever was. Northward, an
even plain stretches until the rising of the next hill,
on which is Chûn Castle. This open space is unbroken by hedges, and not a tree or a bush is to be seen
— a fitting site for a battle-field, and as such it was
most probably used; for is not the ground spread
with mounds and barrows covering the dust of
ancient warriors. Southward are traces of mystic
circles (one consisting of upright stones, like those
previously noticed, is nearly entire), holed stones,
and other evident signs of the former presence of the
Druids. Near the circle is Cairn Vrês, the "rock of
judgment," with a rock bason on its summit. A barrow near this was opened, when a perfectly walled
grave was found, containing an urn; this grave was
not covered again, and it may still be seen; it is
about six feet long and four feet wide in the middle
— for it is contracted near the extremities. This
barrow covers several such graves. In another part
of the parish a barrow was opened; a " kistvaen " was
in the centre, in which was an ornamented urn, with
several others placed side by side around it, being
fifty altogether. As the Romans buried their dead
in this manner, such places have been attributed to
them; but most of the urns found in Cornwall are of

too rude a character for such a refined people. The accompanying cut represents some which have been found in this district. The largest, which was dug

SEPULCHRAL URNS.

up near the base of a tall granite pillar in the parish of Paul, is about nineteen inches high; the smallest is five inches high, and ornamented in a manner common to the British. These urns may be seen in the museum at Penzance.

The barren plain below Cairn Kenidzhek is called the Gump*, — a well-known haunt of the fairies. The benighted traveller has been oft led astray here, and has beheld the most wonderful sights — has been conducted hence into the shadowy regions of fairyland; the "little people" have tuned him harmonious music on heath-bells, have danced around him

* Cornish for "a plain."

in a mystic circle, shown him bright lights, and beguiled his senses, leaving him alone on the dewy ground at the grey dawn, when they "hear the morning lark."

Fairy legends are yet preserved in the memory of the people; and though we may not meet with anyone who has himself actually seen the "little people," yet many tell of those who have. An old man of the neighbourhood, not long "passed away," is said to have been fully convinced of the reality of a fairy scene which he asserted he once beheld. He was wending his way along one of the rude paths that crosses the Gump. It was a beautiful summer's evening, the "Hooting Cairn" was silent; for not a breath of wind passed over the plain. The sun had gone down beyond the sea-line, and the purple and golden mists of evening were blending into a sober grey, an indistinct twilight. Chûn Cromlêh stood dark and shadowy on the brow of the hill, the huge shape of the castle also seemed more imposing in the uncertain light, and the dew was silently descending on the heath and furze. The old man steadily continued his course, musing, perhaps, on the legends of the spot, and anxious to reach a more frequented road, when there arose on the air a sound of the sweetest music—a soft, a lovely melody, like the breathings of an Æolian harp. He looked around him, but nothing uncommon met his gaze. Still the mysterious sound continued, and he stood lost in bewilderment. The depth of twilight was increasing, and he was yet many a step from home. But the

music had an irresistible charm about it, which
tempted him to seek whence it came.   So he stepped
aside from the path, and proceeding a little way, on
a spot where the turf was smoother than elsewhere,
the most wonderful and enchanting scene was before
him.   There *were* fairies and no mistake.   Scores
of them were here assembled, holding a fair.   A band
of musicians was at that moment taking the most
prominent part in the proceedings; lustily they blew
the pipes and tuned their instruments, producing
melodious sounds that no mortal could imitate.
There were stalls beautifully and temptingly laid out,
and graceful arches and garlands were woven with
the flowers that the tract afforded.   The fairies wore
but little dress; some had heath-bells jauntily stuck
on their heads; some donned the golden blossoms of
the furze, which looked like helmets.   The old
man's curiosity was excited, and he wished to approach yet nearer.   So he lay down and dragged
himself cautiously towards them, watching their
gambols and listening to the music, with which he
could find no fault, although leader of the village
choir.   In the mean time the fairies were continually
increasing in number; but they were not seen until
they alighted on the spot.   Some dropped from the
wing of a bat as it dashed along; and other winged
creatures of the night brought their riders to the fair.
But the gems and wonderful little articles which
glistened on the stalls chiefly attracted attention;
they were marvellously made.   The old man had a
longing desire to possess some, so he threw his hat

amongst the company, and made a dash at the coveted treasures; but when he took up his hat nothing was to be seen on the spot but a few snails creeping over the moist grass, and the gossamer threads bespangled with dew-drops.

A weird tract is that of Kenidzhek and the Gump, and of ill repute. The old half-starved horses on the common, with their hides grown rusty brown, like dried and withered grass, by exposure, are ridden by the arch-fiend at night. He is said to hunt lost souls over this heath; and an old stile hard by bears an evil name, for there the souls are sure to be caught, none being able to get over it. The people tell of midnight fights by demons, and of a shadowy form holding a lantern to the combatants.

The very word, Kenidzhek, "*the Hooting Cairn*," is ominous, and fearful and melancholy sounds does the wind make in passing around its jagged buttresses. Even by day it imparts a gloomy and mysterious impression; by night, the miners cross the Gump in fear and trembling.

CHAP. VII.

THE valley of Gulval opens from the sterile and bleak region of the north. As it approaches the south it becomes suddenly beautiful and more highly cultivated, is clothed with luxuriant masses of foliage; cooling shades are formed by the river's side, whose course is crossed by rustic bridges, and wild flowers of various hues profusely adorn its banks and slopes.

Starting from the southern coast, just beyond the sand and pebbles of the beach will be seen a grass peculiar to the spot, the *Cynodon Dactylon*, which is here figured in company with the quaking grass, *Briza minor*, also found in this parish. The latter is a most graceful plant; its triangular spikelets appear to be always in motion, and tremble with the gentlest breeze.

Along this shore grow *Kalystegia Soldanella,*
Euphorbia Paralias, and *Euphorbia Peplis;* the
last, however, is rarely to be met with.

CYNODON DACTYLON, AND BRIZA MINOR.

At the eastern portion of the marsh, between
Penzance and Marazion, *Litorella lacustris* and *Pilu-*
laria globulifera may be found. Many species of
algæ have been discovered at Long Rock, sometimes

thrown on the sand after storms, as, *Stilophora rhizodes, Asperococcus compressus, Sphacelaria filicina, Ectocarpus Hincksiæ, Naccaria Wigghii, Microcladia glandulosa, Halymenia ligulata, Nitophyllum Hilliæ, Bonnemaisonia asparagoides,* &c. In autumn the leaves of Zostera are covered with the beautiful *Ceramium fastigiatum.*

Chyandour, "the house by the water," although beyond the borough bounds, immediately adjoins Penzance. The Messrs. Bolitho have an extensive establishment here for the smelting of tin. The Prince Consort honoured these works with a visit in the year 1846, and partook of beefsteaks fried on the hot blocks of tin.

Following the pathway fields from Ponsandane, "the man's bridge," and not failing to notice the charming prospect of Pendrea on the left, we arrive at the parish church, which is embowered in trees, and, with the surrounding cottages, forms the most picturesque and truly rustic village in the district. Some of the cottages may be observed overspread with the scarlet geranium, and the myrtle grows well in the gardens. These, and many plants which in other parts of England are delicately reared in greenhouses, flourish in the open air all the year round in this neighbourhood.

The churchyard is truly English. Where shall we find such spots as this save in our native land? surrounded by elms and dark fir trees, some of which lean toward the church, casting their shadows across the grey old tower, over the "grassy mounds" and moss-covered tombstones. The graves are not set rigidly in straight lines, as in modern cemeteries, but each on some favourite or selected site. They are not walked over as pleasure ground by holiday seekers, nor formally arranged in flower-beds: the

GULVAL.

green sod flourishes here undisturbed; enriched by the falling leaves of autumn it rises up afresh in the spring-time. Beneath the shade of the trees and the church, can there be a more fitting resting-place for those who have " fallen asleep? "

The church, an unpretending structure, has recently been reseated and otherwise restored, and a new stained-glass window decorates the east end.

On the wall in the belfry is the following quaint rhyme : —

> " Good Sirs! our meaning is not small
> That, God to Praise, assemblies call;
> And warn the sluggard, when at home,
> That he may with devotion come
> Unto the Church, and joyn in prayer;
> Of Absolution take his share.
> Who hears the bells, appears betime,
> And in his seat against we chime.
> Therefore I'd have you not to vapour,
> Nor blame ye lads that use ye clapper
> By which are scar'd the fiends of Hell,
> And all by virtue of a Bell."

The frames of the bells bear the date of 1600, the south bell 1640, the middle bell has no inscription or date, the remaining one, however, is thus inscribed : —

"ILE . RING . ALLWAYS . MY . MAKERS . PRAYES."   1675.

Between each word is stamped the head of Charles II. with the superscription " Carolus II. Dei Gratia," like a coin of the period, and about the size of a shilling. A curious old cross stands in the eastern part of the churchyard.

In the taxation of Pope Nicholas this parish is called Lamieschi, and in another manuscript Lanesely. *Lan*, a church, and *shei*, low or lower, — the *low church*, as a writer remarks, agrees with its situation very well. It was dedicated to St. Gudwall, or Gunwall, a Briton, who was born in Wales about the year 500 : he collected eighty-eight monks in a little island called Plecit, which was no more than a rock surrounded by water, leaving this he came into Cornwall by sea. He was afterwards bishop of Brittany.

There was a famous spring called " Gulfwell," south of the church, much resorted to for the purposes of divination.

To investigate the rural charms of this locality, it matters little which road is taken, for something will be found in all to interest and delight. There are picturesque old mills, rustic bridges, and many pretty "bits" which afford agreeable subjects for the sketcher. If a more extensive scene be desired, let him visit Gulval Cairn, a pile of rock, about a quarter of a mile from the church, climb to its highest part, and behold the outstretched bay ; on the right lies the town and harbour of Penzance ; on the left the famed St. Michael's ; betwixt these, in the middle distance, the pinnacles of the tower we have just left peep above the surrounding foliage ; in the foreground rise the massive rocks of the cairn, partially overspread with ivy ; and at their base low thick bushes. This is said to have been a favourite resort of Sir Humphry Davy in his youthful days, and we may travel far before we meet with a picture combining so many objects of interest in such a splendid setting.

Among other cryptogamous plants which clothe the rocks of this cairn, are *Jungermannia Mackaii* and *J. fragifolia*.

The greater part of the south of this parish is cultivated as garden ground, and the pathways by the gardens and orchards are of the most pleasing description; the lover of nature will here find much to engage his attention. The extreme fertility of this locality is partly owing to its nearness to the sea, seaweed and sand being so easily procured. The latter appears to have been valued at an early period, for during "the time of Richard, King of the Romans, and Earl of Cornwall, a grant was made to the Cornishmen to take sand freely out of the sea, and carry it through the whole county, to manure their ground withal, which grant was confirmed by Henry III. This must have been one of their chief ways of improving their land, or there had been no occasion to apply for that grant, which was certainly occasioned by the exactions of owners of land on the sea coast."

On the high road from Chyandour to Trevaylor, a rutted and straggling lane on the right leads down to Bleu (parish) Bridge, at one end of which is a pillar of granite, about six feet high, bearing this inscription "Quenatavus Icdinui filius." It was erected, perhaps, to some chief or noble who might have fallen here in battle. From the character of the letters its date has been fixed about the end of the sixth century. This monument for some time served as the stepping stone of the bridge; to preserve it, the proprietor of the land very properly caused it to be placed in its present position. The spot would be well worthy of a visit, had there been no ancient monument there: it is a gem of rural

BLEU BRIDGE.

scenery. There is a long vista of lofty arching elms, with a glimpse of a white cottage through the openings between the trunks; a clear stream with tall and graceful weeds on its banks, and the rude foot-bridge with its iron rail, are pleasingly arranged; indeed, nothing more is to be desired to complete the picture.

The old seat of Kenegie, "the mossy hedge," in this parish occupies a fine situation. Another residence is called Rosemorran, "the vale of blackberries," a name it justly merits; the house is almost entirely hidden by trees on which the rooks build and quarrel, filling the air with their noisy cawing. On a hedge here is an ancient cross; it was most probably removed hither from some other site.

It is a pleasant path across the fields from Rosemorran to Trevaylor, "the workman's place." A babbling brook is crossed that rises in the Zennor hills, and winds its way down this lovely valley, known by the name of "Trevaylor Bottoms," rich in tangled underwood; the trailing bramble and the woodbine twine together along the ground, and over the old moss-covered trunks; a little farther on are the golden gorse and purple heath, spreading their bright masses of colour over the green turf. Here

" Nature's hand has wildly strewn her flowers ; "

and many elegant varieties present themselves, amongst which may be found *Zygodon conoideus, Z. viridissimus, Hookeria lucens, Daltonia heteromalla, Wahlenbergia hederacea, Viola lactea, Exacum filiforme, Bartsia viscosa,* and other beautiful little plants which love such sheltered and secluded haunts. In the stream is *Fontinalis squamosa,* and the stones are fringed with the rare moss *Hypnum flagellare.* At this place, also, grows the rare *Jungermannia calyptrifolia.* In the bogs here, and generally throughout the district, *Pinguicula Lusitanica,* pale butterwort, is frequently met with.

PINGUICULA LUSITANICA.

The flowers, of a delicate pink colour, are attached to slender stalks from two to three inches high; although this plant makes little show, and might be passed unheeded, on inspection it will be found of the most elegant and graceful construction; the leaves are doubled up at the sides and veined in a curious manner. From their greasy nature the plant derives its name.

At Trevaylor an avenue of trees forms a noble archway over the high road—the rooks have possession of the upper boughs. A very large ash, in an adjoining pathway field, is the finest tree of the kind in the west of Cornwall. The ash was formerly abundant in this part of the county, and some give the present name of the hundred, Penwith, as the "head of the ash trees." The small-leaved elm is doubtless a native of Cornwall.

One of the most extensive views of Mount's Bay is from the terrace-walk at Trevaylor; seven or eight of the surrounding parish churches are visible from this spot. An ancestor of the present proprietor was the first Protestant vicar of Gulval.

Instead of continuing on the road to New Mill, we ascend the high ground on the right to inspect some curious enclosures, but on the opposite hill, just above the farm place of Chysauster, " the dwelling on the south," are more important remains — supposed to have been ancient British residences.* They consist of rude walls, indifferently put together without cement, and were probably covered with poles and reeds, or some of the tangled brushwood, which might then have been easily collected ; — such were the structures which afforded sufficient shelter for our hardy forefathers. On this hill are the ruins of seven or eight of these huts, some in a better state

* In the Archæological Journal, vol. xviii., I have given a fuller account of these huts.

of preservation than others. From the most entire
the accompanying plan is made, and as they were
nearly all alike, it will serve to show their general
construction; first there is an elliptical thick wall,
faced externally and internally with stones: within
its breadth are four compartments, I., II., III., IV.
In these the stones overlap each other a little as they
approach the top, giving to each somewhat the ap-

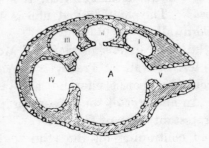

pearance of a bee-hive; examples of this mode of
building will also be found in some of the ancient
caves of the district. The centre of the hut is
occupied by a large open space A, from which are
entrances into the smaller divisions alluded to; this
area probably served to secure the cattle from
marauders, or for a number of men to assemble
together in times of danger. The entrance, V, faces
south-east.

These curious structures are surrounded by numerous *gurgos*, broken-down fences, forming enclosures
of fantastic shapes. A little way down the hill side
are terraces, formed by the ground being levelled;

the turf over these is beautifully smooth, and they are in a great measure free from furze and brambles, which so plentifully overgrow the old walls above, and appear to have been made for some games or amusements rather than for any service in warfare. On the hill-side too, is an ancient cave similar to those of Bolleit and Pendeen. As these huts agree with the descriptions given of British dwellings, it is most probable they were erected in very primitive times. The habits of the Cornu-Britons were simple; but though wild in their manners, we learn that they highly respected the laws of hospitality. Very little is known of their domestic arrangements, but it seems they baked their bread upon stones called *gredles;* venison was cooked on beds of flaming fern, and covered with smooth flat stones, then another layer of ferns; a similar practice existed in the Highlands of Scotland; thus dressed, venison is said to have a peculiar and pleasant flavour. There were some birds and fish which, from religious or superstitious motives, they abstained from eating. Skins of beasts served them for beds. Their sports were hunting, fowling, and hurling. They had flocks and herds; the tracts of land around their castles were of great extent, " and here," says a writer, " might shepherds have ranged with their flocks, or labourers have tilled the ground." According to Diodorus Siculus, the Britons, when they had reaped their corn, by cutting the ear from the stubble, were accustomed to lay it up for preservation in subterranean caves; it is not improbable that the cave mentioned might have been so used. They knew how to make butter, but its use was appropriated to the more delicate palates of the nobles. The moose, which they called the *segh*, or savage deer, was hunted by powerful dogs; these were the large southern hounds, hence called "segh-dogs." Other objects of the chase were the bull, the boar, and the bear.

How wonderful seem to us the changes wrought in the course of time, when standing amidst such ruins as these, — forming a link between the far past and the present.

Castle-an-dinas, the embankments and ditches of which may yet be traced, is on the same hill, a mile to the east. It occupies the highest ground in the district, being 735 feet above the sea, and commands an extensive view, extending to both channels. It will be noticed that the ancient village of Chysauster, like that of Chûn, is placed under the protection of a fortification. They are each, also, near a cromlêh — that of Mulfra stands on high land, the left side of the Zennor road; its covering stone has slipped from its supporters. Dr. Borlase says the stones for this monument were evidently brought from a cairn or ledge of rocks below, about a furlong to the north-west. Mulfra signifies "a round bald hill."

Beyond this hill the road divides — that which branches off to the right leads to Zennor, "holy land," the other to Morvah, "the place by the sea." Morvah church is comparatively a new building, of a plain character, occupying a dreary and exposed situation. Proceeding in a direct line from the church to the sea, we shall come on the course of a little stream, which dashes over the cliff in a style worthy of a mountain torrent— it leaps into a fearful abyss shut in by lofty cliffs — yet not so perpendicular but that they may be descended, although it is a dangerous and toilsome task. But only at the base can the waterfall be properly seen; jumping from rock to rock, disappearing occasionally behind some huge mass — then bursting forth in sparkling foam through the next opening—rushing among the loose stones, and making music as it goes, until it blends with the spray of the waves.

It was as fine an autumn morning as could be desired, when I started with a friend from Penzance for the purpose of sketching this fall. We had reached the highest part of Morvah down, which commands a view of both channels, when, instead of beholding the horizon of the North Sea, which we naturally expected to meet our gaze, we found every-thing obscured by a thick white mist, which was slowly but surely spreading over the land. It was truly a strange sight, for on turning to the south, Mount's Bay was seen below sparkling in sunshine, clear and bright, — it almost appeared like the boundary of another world; but we were soon enveloped in clouds. As this was rather unpleasant for walking in, we took shelter for some time in a cottage. And here it should be noticed how hospitable are the dwellers in these Cornish cottages to strangers in emergencies of this kind; the best polished chairs are immediately

brought forward, and you are welcome to whatever
the house affords. Generally, it will be observed
that everything is scrupulously clean, both within and
without; the housewife considers it an important
duty to whitewash the wall around the door and
window every Saturday; this is especially the case
with miners' and fishermen's cots : the room is sure
to be decorated with pictures, cheap, old-fashioned
coloured prints of the worst description, generally of
a religious character, such as Daniel in the lions' den
or some more sacred subject. These, however, are regarded with the greatest reverence, and afford the
simple owners as much pleasure as a connoisseur
would feel in the presence of a cartoon by Raffaelle.
To return to our sketching expedition. In a little
while the mist disappeared as rapidly as it had come
on, and we soon arrived at the head of the gorge
through which the stream finds its way to the sea.
After much difficulty we descended to the bottom of
the fall, a depth of full two hundred feet, and com-
menced operations with the pencil. All went on well
for about an hour, and the sketches were proceeding
rapidly, when, almost in an instant, the scene was once
more hid from sight. The mist, denser than before,
had come on again; as our backs were to the sea we
had not noticed its approach. Our materials were
soon packed, and after a fearful scramble we regained
the summit, and there was no help for it but to walk
back, a distance of about eight miles, and not a
sheltered road by any means. The fog soon turned
into downright rain. Our converse by the way was

not lively, what was said was chiefly in monosyllables, and when we reached the town we were drenched to the skin, and our sketches had become "dissolving views." Such is the uncertainty of the atmosphere around the Land's End coast. Strangers especially often remark it; and after a visitor has been in the neighbourhood a little while he rarely ventures far without an umbrella. A gloomy morning often turns out the finest day, whilst a beautiful morning, which tempts the tourist from home and shelter, leaves him to wend his way back miserably drenched.

Northward is Porth Moina, the Monk's Port, formed on one side by the headland called Bosigran Castle. Porth Moina was probably the landing-place of some Irish saint. In their zeal for the welfare of the Cornish, no obstacle prevented them from crossing the channel. St. Patrick himself is said to have crossed on a stone altar. Lesser saints came on millstones and other articles which in these degenerate days refuse to swim. These miraculous perform-ances must have had a great effect on the minds of the Cornish. At one place in the county there is a well springing from a rock which, tradition says, has flowed ever since one of these holy men struck the spot with his staff to quench his ass's thirst.

Remains of the old fortification at Bosigran may yet be seen. The rocks here are granite, and have a pale reddish tint; when lit up by the setting sun they have a lovely and brilliant appearance. This is one of the finest pieces of cliff scenery on the north coast of the

district. Standing on the rugged crags an oft-quoted
passage might fairly be repeated here—

> "How fearful
> And dizzy 'tis, to cast one's eyes so low!
> The crows and choughs, that wing the midway air,
> Show scarce so gross as beetles; half-way down
> Hangs one that gathers samphire, dreadful trade!
> Methinks he seems no bigger than his head."

It is not, however, such a "dreadful trade," here
to gather the samphire, which is found plentifully

SAMPHIRE.

all round the coast. An engraving of the samphire,
Crithmum maritinum, is here introduced. *Sali-*

cornia herbacea, a plant which grows in salt marshes, is often pickled for real samphire, but it is very inferior and quite destitute of the true flavour. *Inula Hellenium* is found in this parish.

Around the bleak hills and towering cliffs in this locality, various hawks may generally be seen hovering about; the peregrine falcon, or cliff hawk, has been captured here; the blue rock dove, and Baillon's crake, have also been procured from this parish.

Bosigran is just under Cairn Galva, whose boldly-formed outline is distinctly seen to the east. Crossing Haldeen, "the bramble moor," the junction of the granite and slate will be observed near Porthmear Cove, "exhibiting the most beautiful and instructive illustration of the curious phenomena usually observable at the points of union of the slate with the fundamental granite."

The Gurnard's Head projects considerably into the sea in a northerly direction : it is one of the finest and most romantic points on the north side of the Land's End, and "affords an excellent illustration of the nature of stratification in general, and is the clearest example of the general characters of that particular assemblage of rocks which immediately repose on the granite in this part of Cornwall." The late Davies Gilbert was so struck with the appearance of this bold formation, that he purchased the estate for the purpose of acquiring the property of a mass of rocks so geologically interesting. The ancient name of the headland is Treryn Dinas, for this was fortified like

the other principal promontories. It is called the
"Gurnard's Head," from some fanciful resemblance

THE GURNARD'S HEAD.

to that fish. On the isthmus are the remains of a
small chapel; the altar stone, a flat slab of granite,
is still entire; there was a holy well close by. Probably the hermits who occupied these sea-side cells,
selected such spots that they might be at hand to
succour and relieve the shipwrecked mariner. This
custom of men withdrawing themselves from the
world to lead lives of contemplation and seclusion,
forms an interesting feature of the middle ages, and
though such modes of life would not be suitable to
the present time, these "pious men of eld" claim
our respect, and were extremely useful at the period
in which they lived; the wayfarer, the poor and
the needy were sure of their sympathy, and were

always welcome to what assistance these solitaries could afford. There are memories of the "olden time" which almost incite regret at the changes that centuries have wrought.

Seine-boats are kept in the adjoining cove, and fish cellars are erected on the cliff above. A fine raised beach here is worthy of inspection.

The botanist may discover *Gentiana campestris*, at the Gurnard's Head; on this coast also is found *Trigonella ornithopodioides* and *Pycnothelia papillaria*.

Continuing round the shore the scenes are varied and pleasing, but of a very different character from the granite cliffs on the south, still each point and tract has its Cornish name, such as Ros-an-hale, " river on the heath;" Cairn Mên Porthglâs, " Green cove;" Carmellow rock; Veor (great) Cove; Pendour ("the head of the water") Cove; a stream here finds its way over rocks and through tall weeds, and just before meeting the ocean falls over the wheel of a picturesque old mill, romantically situated on the cliff.

Zennor church, about a quarter of a mile distant, is a plain, weather-beaten structure, quite in keeping with the adjacent country. It is said to have been dependent on St. Michael's Mount, and the bells bear inscriptions to the effect that they were presented by the prior of the Mount. The font is worthy of notice; it is probably of Late Decorated architecture, *circa* 1390, or a little earlier. Some of the bench-ends were carved; on one is the strange figure of a mermaid, which to many might seem out of character in a church. "The fishermen who

MILL AT PENDOUR COVE, ZENNOR.

were the ancestors of the Church came from the Galilæan waters to haul for men. We, born to God at the font, are children of the water. Therefore all the early symbolism of the Church was of and from the sea. The carvure of the early arches was taken from the sea and its creatures. Fish, dolphins, mermen and mermaids redound in the early types transferred to wood and stone."*

FONT IN ZENNOR CHURCH.

In the churchyard is the following epitaph:—

" Hope, fear, false-joy, and trouble,
    Are these four winds which daily toss this bubble.
    His breath's a vapour, and his life's a span,
    'Tis glorious misery to be born a man."

A few yards north of the church there is a logan

* R.S.H.

rock, about eighteen feet long, with rock basons
on its surface. To the east rise rocky granite hills;
on the nearest the cairns are of a remarkable
character, the rocks being piled up in regular flat

BENCH-END IN ZENNOR CHURCH.

layers; some are very nicely poised, whilst others
lean in wonderful positions. More eccentric piles of
granite are not to be found in the west of Cornwall.
On this range is the Zennor Cromlêh, the largest in
the county.

The wild tract spreading away to the north-east is
the parish of Towednack. Along the coast it is
skirted with slate rocks, but the interior is granite,

large masses of which are scattered and strewn upon the heaths and crofts. A few miners' cottages are dotted here and there over this dreary region, but they cannot be said to give it a more cheerful aspect. The grey church blends with the monotonous tone of the country, and seems to have been subject to few such alterations as have disfigured many old

TOWEDNACK CHURCH.

churches. It possesses a true chancel arch — a rare feature in the churches of Cornwall. This arch is Early English, and dates, perhaps, about 1220; the rest of the church is Late.

For the following remarks on this church I am indebted to Mr. Edward Godwin, architect:—
"Towednack church consists of nave, chancel, south aisle continuing as a south chapel to chancel, south

porch and tower at west end.   The south aisle and
porch are additions of the eighteenth century.   The
view of the north side shows that even here the idea
of continuity was not lost sight of.   All the windows,
with the exception of the belfry lights, are modern.
There is a rudely constructed north doorway, the
head segmental, cut out of one stone.   The belfry
lights are square headed and chamfered : below the
cill of the east window is a bold string-course.   The
cornice and string-course, though plain are very
effective, and in harmony with the rugged desolation
of the spot.   Indeed, there are few churches which
maintain this principle better than the little church
of Towednack, and herein it is an admirable lesson
to modern architects, who are often too apt to design,

CHANCEL ARCH.

not churches only, but every class of building, without
paying sufficient attention to the natural characteristics of the site.   Internally the church is disappoint-
ing, owing to the churchwardenic application of

plaster and whitelime.* The roof is concealed by a
segmental pointed ceiling, which cuts off the apex of
the chancel arch ; this latter, as will be seen from
the sketch, is of two chamfered orders, continuous
and corbelled. The tower arch was originally of one
plain soffit ; a late pair of responds and an inner
chamfered order has been added : a portion of the
old impost moulding remains. The tower stairs are
of a rather unusual plan, no newel or winders being
used, and the entrance being direct from the nave.

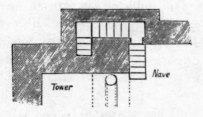

PLAN OF TOWER STAIRS.

The old square-headed doorways remain, but the old
floor has been removed and a later one substituted at
a higher level."

Two bench-ends in the nave are worthy of notice ;
They bear very Spanish-looking, medallion portraits,
moustached, bearded and hatted ; they are dated
1633, and have inscribed on them, the letters inter-

* This plaster, however, will afford compensation to the botanist.
as it encourages the growth of a rare alga, *Oscillatoria cyanea.* It
grows here abundantly, clothing the walls with a beautiful light sky-
blue colour.

laced in a singular manner, the names of "James Trewhela, warden," "Master Matthew Trenwith, warden." The remnant of the chancel screen is of the same age. In the porch there is a block of granite forming a seat, on which is inscribed a cross of a simple, though rather unusual, form. The old sextoness told me it was the stem of a cross, of which the plinth may yet be seen near the eastern entrance to the churchyard.

Borlase figures a logan rock in this parish. There was also a large rock, called the "Giant's Rock," supported by four pillars; beneath it was found an urn and several coins of the Roman Emperors.

Returning to the coast many fine bits of scenery may yet be noticed. Between the Carlow Rocks and Wicca Cove are curious veins of granite. The Carracks, "rocks," are off the shore. Another rock beyond the cliffs has a strange legend attached to it, relating to some Lady Sibbet, or Sybella, who used to swim to it and back again every morning.

Many of the points bear names similar to those already passed, such as Clodgy Point, Cairn du, Polmear.

The parish of Lelant* adjoins Towednack. Lelant church, dedicated to St. Uny, is chiefly interesting for its early Norman remains, which consist of an entire arch, pier, and respond of the second bay on

---

* The slopes and banks between Lelant and St. Ives are very beautiful from the abundance of blue, red, and white varieties of columbine, *Aquilegia vulgaris.* Near St. Ives may be found *Statice Dodartii* and *Orobanche barbata.*

the north side of the nave. Immediately adjoining, there is a fine sharp-pointed arch, of the beginning of the thirteenth century.

NORMAN ARCH, LELANT.

This Norman arch is the only remaining work of that period to be found in any of the churches of the district; some churches in other parts of the county, however, still retain very excellent examples of Norman architecture. The beautiful doorways and arches at Morwenstow and Kilkhampton may be instanced, as well as the noble west front of St. Germans. Tintagel may be referred to the same period. There are also Norman doorways at Manaccan, St. Anthony in Roseland, St. Cleer, Landewednack, &c. The last is figured in "A Week at the Lizard," by the Rev. C. A. Johns.

At Ludgvan, Dr. Borlase, the antiquary of Cornwall, long resided, and his monument may be seen in the church. His name is thus inscribed on one of

the bells, "Wm. Borlase, Rector, 1722." Another
bell bears this motto—"Soli Deo gloria," "Pax in
terris." The font in this church is worthy of notice,
it is surrounded with the tooth moulding, a peculiar
feature in the early English style.

FONT IN LUDGVAN CHURCH.

The patron saint of a well at Ludgvan laid this
peculiar spell on the water, that whoever should be
baptized with it should never come to the ignominious
end of being hanged, consequently a Ludgvan man
has never suffered this disgrace; and it is farther
reported, that the inhabitants of neighbouring
parishes have been seen carrying off bottles of the

water that their children might have the benefit of its efficacy.

St. Ives with its noble bay and fine old church, comes on the boundary of the Land's End district : so does the lofty St. Michael's : —

> " He whose brow
> Is crown'd with castles, and whose rocky sides
> Are clad with dusky ivy."

This island rock with its ancient monastery and castled summit, cannot be properly handled in a hasty sketch; to show its beauties and to tell its story may be the object of a future volume.

To enjoy the western cliffs, one should stay at the locality for some days, or weeks, if possible ; be on the spot at all hours, see the mists of morning clearing away from the headlands and the sea; behold the sparkling of the waves in the noonday sun, and the golden and mellow tints of evening when all is calm and peaceful.

Those who wish to behold nature in her grandest aspect, those who love the sea breezes, and the flowers which grow by the cliffs, the cairns and monumental rocks, all hoary and bearded with moss, those who are fond of the legends and traditions of old, and desire to tread on ground sacred to the peculiar rites and warlike deeds of remote ages, should visit the land of Old Cornwall, of which it will be found that the district of Bolerium is not the least interesting portion.

INDEX.

INDEX.

PLANTS.

Phænogamous or Flowering Plants.

Ferns.

INDEX.

MOSSES.

HEPATICÆ.

LICHENS.

ALGÆ.

THE END.